BOOK OF
DINOSAURS
MICHAEL BENTON

POCKET

BOOK OF
DINOSAURS

MICHAEL BENTON

KINGFISHER BOOKS

Kingfisher Books, Grisewood & Dempsey Ltd,
Elsley House, 24–30 Great Titchfield Street,
London W1P 7AD

First published in hardcover in 1984.
This edition published in 1987

Reprinted 1988, 1990

BRITISH LIBRARY CATALOGUING IN PUBLICATION DATA
Benton, Michael
  Pocket book of dinosaurs.
  (Kingfisher pocket books)
  1. Dinosaurs—Juvenile literature
  I. Title   II. Benton, Michael. Kingfisher
  pocket book of dinosaurs
  567.9'1   QE862.D5

  ISBN 0-86272-273-X

Edited by Kate Hayden
Designed by Ben White
Cover design by the Pinpoint Design Company
Illustrations by Jim Channell, John Gosler,
Bernard Robinson, David·Webb
Printed in Spain

Contents

Introduction

What is a Dinosaur?

The dinosaurs ruled the world for over 160 million years. The last dinosaurs died out 65 million years ago, many years before the first humans evolved – about 160 million years ago. Dinosaurs were a special group of prehistoric *reptiles* and their closest living relations are the crocodiles and birds. The dinosaurs lived on land and they were nearly all big – the longest were as long as ten cars parked nose to tail, the tallest could have looked over the roof of a three storey building. At the other extreme there were dinosaurs no bigger than a turkey. In between there were dinosaurs of all shapes and sizes, most of them completely different from anything we know today.

Yet nothing was known about these extraordinary creatures until the 19th century. It was only then that people realized that dinosaurs had ever existed. Since then thousands of *skeletons* have been collected all over the world.

How Many Different Dinosaurs Were There?

It is difficult to estimate how many different *species* of dinosaur have been found. Early dinosaur collectors often named the dinosaurs they found without checking if the skeleton was really different from all those that had previously been discovered. In some cases, rival teams of bone hunters made up new names for everything they found. This could lead to confusion when the rival teams were collecting similar skeletons. For example, in the late 19th century, one American scientist named the huge 'thunder lizard' BRONTOSAURUS. It was later found that a rival scientist had already named another skeleton of the same animal as APATOSAURUS and this name is now used because it was given first. Many extra names have also been invented for similar dinosaurs found in different parts of the world.

If we combine all the names that have been given to similar dinosaurs we have a total of about 250 species. But some of these may be based on just a few fragments of bone or a single tooth! In the end, we have a number of about 150 'good' dinosaurs. Most of these are shown in the dictionary in this book.

▶ **Preparing the shoulder blade** of the giant sauropod dinosaur *Camarasaurus*, at Dinosaur National Monument, near Vernal, Utah, USA. One of the best known dinosaur sites in the world.

Time and Place

The 150 species of dinosaur did not all live at the same time. Dinosaur bones are found in rocks of different ages, varying from 220 to 65 million years old. Very often, several different animals may be found together in a single rock *formation*, and we may guess that they lived together as a *fauna*. When two faunas contain the same forms we can assume that they are of approximately the same age. If we follow the sequences of dinosaur faunas through time, we can see how they *evolved*. Individual *genera* changed their appearance over time, and faunas changed when new types of dinosaurs replaced others.

THESE ARE NOT DINOSAURS

Dimetrodon
(4m long)

What is not a Dinosaur?

Since dinosaurs only lived on land, many prehistoric animals cannot be considered dinosaurs. In the air were the *pterosaurs*, a separate group of gliding and flying reptiles which ranged in size from a crow to an aeroplane (wingspans of up to 10 metres across). Two large groups of reptiles ruled the sea during the age of the dinosaurs: the *ichthyosaurs* and the *plesiosaurs*. These animals were not closely related to the dinosaurs or to each other.

Other well-known prehistoric animals did not even live at the same time as the dinosaurs. A wide variety of fossil reptiles lived before the dinosaurs came on the scene, including the *mammal-like reptiles*, such as the 'sail lizards'. After the dinosaurs died out, the *mammals* became the most important animals, as they still are today. So, well-known extinct mammals like the mammoth are not dinosaurs either.

Pterosaur
(wingspan 7m)

Ichthyosaur
(3–10m)

Plesiosaur
(7–8m long)

Classification of the Dinosaurs

The dinosaurs are divided into two large groups, or *orders* – the SAURISCHIA (sawr-ISK-eea) and the ORNITHISCHIA (orn-ith-ISK-eea). These names, like most dinosaur names, are derived from Latin and Greek words that describe the animals. Saurischia means 'lizard hip' and Ornithischia means 'bird hip'. These are a kind of short-hand description of the distinguishing features of the dinosaurs in each group. Dinosaurs had three bones in the hip region and they were arranged in two ways:

(1) 'lizard hip' with each of the three bones pointing in a different direction = SAURISCHIA
(2) 'bird hip' with the two lower bones running backwards = ORNITHISCHIA

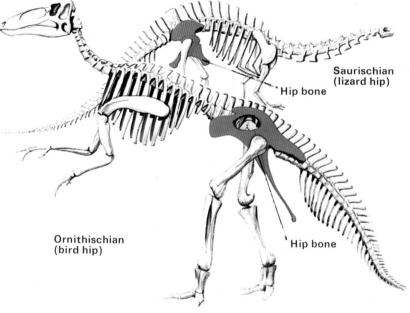

Saurischian
(lizard hip)

Hip bone

Ornithischian
(bird hip)

Hip bone

When a dinosaur skeleton is found it is usually easy to decide to which order it belongs.

When we *classify* dinosaurs, we try to decide how closely they are related to each other. The smallest unit of classification is the *species*, and the largest unit used here is the *order*. In between, there is a series of group names: order, suborder, infraorder, family, genus (plural, genera), species.

As an example, how do we classify the big meat-eating dinosaur **Tyrannosaurus rex**? It is placed in the Order Saurischia because it has a 'lizard hip'. Then, it belongs to the Suborder Theropoda, which includes all the meat-eating dinosaurs. Within the Theropoda TYRANNOSAURUS belongs to the Infraorder Carnosauria – the big meat-eaters – and is placed in the Family Tyrannosauridae, or tyrannosaurids, with a few close relatives. Finally, the genus name is *Tyrannosaurus*, and the species name is *rex*.

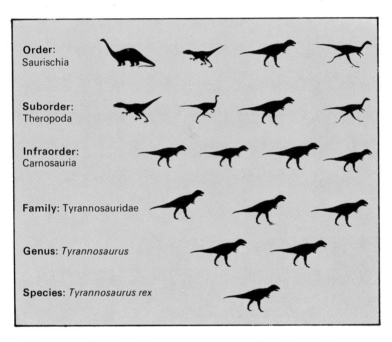

Order: Saurischia

Suborder: Theropoda

Infraorder: Carnosauria

Family: Tyrannosauridae

Genus: *Tyrannosaurus*

Species: *Tyrannosaurus rex*

When we talk about dinosaurs, we normally only use the genus names, because there is often not enough information to decide how to divide them up into species. The species and genus names are written in italics, or underlined, to indicate that the scientific name is being used.

The two big orders of dinosaurs, the Saurischia and Ornithischia, both began at about the same time, 225 million years ago, and died out 65 million years ago. Each group contained many different forms – some of these are shown on pages 14–15. The classification of the main orders, suborders and infraorders of dinosaurs is given on page 176. These names may be found in the dictionary where more detailed information is given.

13

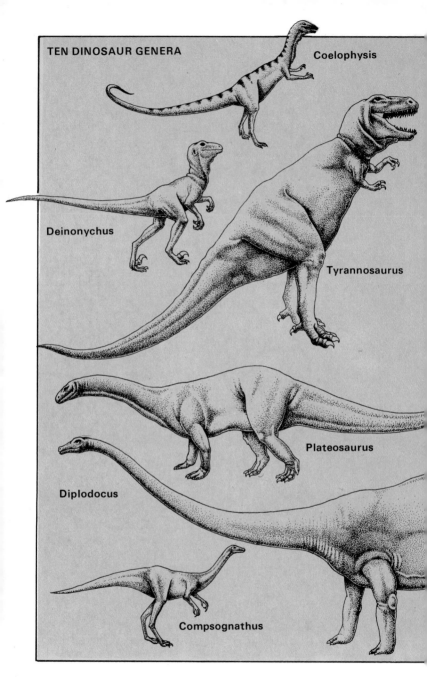

TEN DINOSAUR GENERA

Coelophysis

Deinonychus

Tyrannosaurus

Plateosaurus

Diplodocus

Compsognathus

14

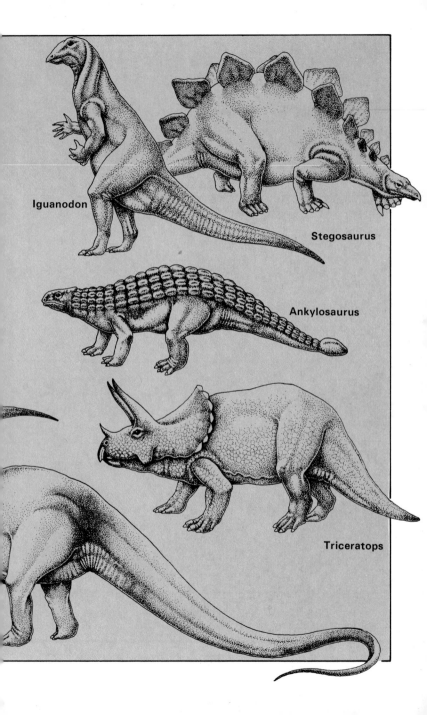

Iguanodon

Stegosaurus

Ankylosaurus

Triceratops

The Age of Dinosaurs

We learn about dinosaurs by studying *fossils*. A fossil is the remains of any ancient plant or animal – usually an *extinct* form. Some fossils appear now only as a vague impression in the rock. Other fossils still have a lot of the original material in them – such as a squashed leaf in coal or a woolly mammoth deep-frozen in the ice of northern Russia. Fossils are not necessarily made of stone; ancient insects preserved in amber are also fossils.

Dinosaurs may be found in several fossil forms but most commonly as footprints and skeletons. Dinosaur skeletons are generally found in sedimentary rocks such as sandstone and mudstone. These fossil skeletons were formed when a dinosaur fell into a lake or river.

HOW A FOSSIL IS FORMED

The body of a dinosaur sinks to the bottom of a river or lake. It may drift with the current.

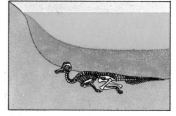

After a while, the flesh is eaten, or it rots, and the skeleton is covered by sand or mud.

Over time, the mud and sand turn into rock. After millions of years, the landscape changes, and the river or lake bed rises.

The rock is worn away by rain and wind, and the dinosaur skeleton is exposed. Somebody may then find it.

Dating the Dinosaurs

The Order of the Rocks

Sedimentary rocks are built up of different layers, rather like a giant cake. As early *palaeontologists* discovered, certain fossils always appear at the same level and fossils in the lower layers are generally simpler and more primitive than the ones higher up. This is because the older rocks lie below the newer rocks and life has evolved from simple to more complicated forms. We can deduce that dinosaurs found in the same layer of rock lived at more or less the same time and at an earlier date than those found in higher layers. There are exceptions to this rule: in some places the Earth has been disturbed and the layers distorted.

▼ **Sedimentary rocks.** In this cliff we can see the beds of sandstone and mudstone that have been laid down one on top of the other over a long period of time. The oldest rocks and fossils are at the bottom.

Telling Geological Time

Today scientists can also tell exactly how old fossils are by measuring *radioactivity*. Certain rocks contain radioactive elements, such as uranium, which break down and give out radioactivity at a steady rate. Over millions of years, the uranium breaks down into lead. Although we cannot usually date the fossils themselves, we can measure the age of the surrounding rocks and guess when the plants and animals lived.

This is how we know that the rocks in which the earliest dinosaurs, such as SALTOPUS and STAURIKOSAURUS are found, were laid down 225 million years ago.

Dinosaurs and the Age of the Earth

Dinosaurs are not the oldest known fossils. They were advanced animals and there had been a long history of life before they evolved. The Earth itself is thought to be 4600 million years old and rocks have been found which are 3800 million years old. The earliest forms of life were simple single cells rather like bacteria. Fossils of these are found in rocks that are 3100 million years old. The oldest fossils of more complicated animals – worms, shellfish, jellyfish, and extinct crab-like animals – date from 'only' 630 million years ago.

As the chart on page 19 shows, these early stages of evolution took longer than the whole period of the evolution of more complex life that has followed since. This period of the first 4000 million years of Earth's history is called the Precambrian (pree-CAM-bree-an). The period of the evolution of complex life after that – the last 600 million years – is called the Phanerozoic (fan-er-oh-ZO-ic: 'visible life').

The Phanerozoic is divided into three main *eras* which are important divisions in the history of life. These eras are the Palaeozoic (pail-ee-oh-ZO-ic: 'ancient life'), the Mesozoic (meez-oh-ZO-ic: 'middle life'), and the Cenozoic (seen-oh-ZO-ic: 'recent life').

In the Palaeozoic (600–245 million years ago), various groups of animals and plants arose, including jellyfish, corals, shellfish, crabs, insects, spiders, fish, amphibians, reptiles, ferns, horsetails, tree-ferns, conifers, and so on. Most of the important animals and plants in the Palaeozoic belonged to groups that are now extinct. In the Mesozoic (245–65 million years ago) some typical modern groups came on the scene, such as birds, mammals and some flowering plants. The dinosaurs ruled the Earth through most of the Mesozoic. In the Cenozoic (65–0 million years ago), we find mammals, birds, insects and flowering plants everywhere, and all the typical modern forms evolved in this time. Humans came on the scene only in the last couple of million years of the Cenozoic.

The Mesozoic is divided into three *periods*, each of which had its own dinosaurs: the Triassic (try-ASS-ic: 245–205 million years ago), The Jurassic (joo-RASS-ic: 205–140 million years ago), and the Cretaceous (cret-AY-shus: 140–65 million years ago). The Triassic period was very important in the history of life. At the start of the Triassic, there were no dinosaurs. The land was ruled by mammal-like reptiles, some of which were as big as hippopotamuses. The mammal-like reptiles died out just before the first dinosaurs appeared near the end of the Triassic. Many lines of dinosaurs evolved in the Jurassic and Cretaceous periods, and they all died out at the end of the Cretaceous.

CHART OF GEOLOGICAL TIME

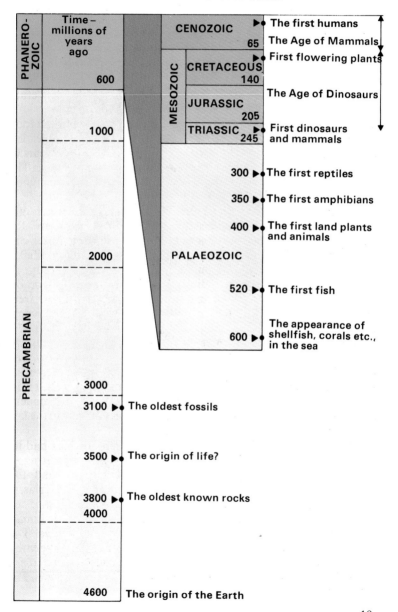

	The first humans	
CENOZOIC		
65	The Age of Mammals	
CRETACEOUS	First flowering plants	
140		
JURASSIC	The Age of Dinosaurs	
205		
TRIASSIC 245	First dinosaurs and mammals	

300 ▸• The first reptiles

350 ▸• The first amphibians

400 ▸• The first land plants and animals

PALAEOZOIC

520 ▸• The first fish

600 ▸• The appearance of shellfish, corals etc., in the sea

3100 ▸• The oldest fossils

3500 ▸• The origin of life?

3800 ▸• The oldest known rocks

4600 The origin of the Earth

PHANERO-ZOIC

Time – millions of years ago

600

1000

2000

3000

4000

PRECAMBRIAN

MESOZOIC

19

The World of the Dinosaurs

If you had looked down on Earth from outer space 200 million years ago, you would not have seen the familiar continents of today. You would have seen a single great land mass. This is because the land masses on the Earth's surface are constantly moving at a rate of a few centimetres a year. At the moment, for instance, North America and Europe are drifting apart very slowly, while North America is drifting towards Russia.

The continents have been drifting in this way for a long time. During the age of the dinosaurs, it happened by chance that nearly all the land masses were joined together. This is very important to consider when we think about how the dinosaurs lived. It would have been easy for herds of dinosaurs to migrate long distances between parts of the world that are now separate, so we are not surprised to find very similar dinosaurs in Africa and North America. The land masses began to drift apart in the later part of the age of the dinosaurs, and the Atlantic and Indian Oceans began to open up.

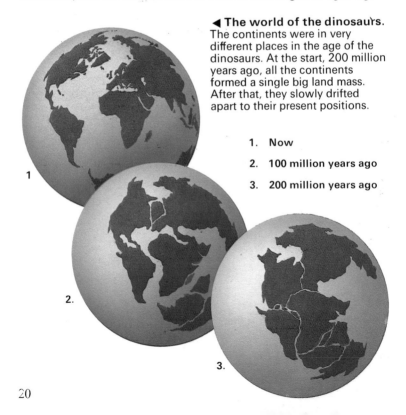

◄ The world of the dinosaurs. The continents were in very different places in the age of the dinosaurs. At the start, 200 million years ago, all the continents formed a single big land mass. After that, they slowly drifted apart to their present positions.

1. Now

2. 100 million years ago

3. 200 million years ago

Climate

The patterns of temperature and winds were also quite different in the age of the dinosaurs. Today there is a great range of temperature between the Equator and the North and South poles. In the Mesozoic, there were no polar ice caps and the range in temperatures worldwide was very small. Because there was realy only one giant land mass in those days, the pattern of winds and weather was probably simpler and more regular than today.

These geographical conditions must have had an effect on the plants and animals of the time, just as the modern plant and animal kingdoms are regulated by present-day conditions. Animals today are usually adapted to certain climates: you will not find Arctic foxes and alligators thriving in the same climate. Sometimes animals are restricted to a particular area by geographical barriers. The vast Indian Ocean prevents kangaroos and koala bears from crossing over to Africa. Most of the dinosaurs, on the other hand, could have lived on land almost anywhere in the world. This is because the climate was fairly uniform and because there were fewer geographical barriers.

Plants and Animals

For most of the Mesozoic, the plants would have seemed strange to us. The early dinosaurs, in the latest part of the Triassic and in the Jurassic, lived in a world of conifers, seed ferns, ferns, horsetails and other 'primitive' plants. Some of these conifers were very like our monkey puzzle trees.

In the middle of the Cretaceous Period, some new plants evolved. These were the familiar flowering plants and trees that we know today. The later dinosaurs then could have fed on plants very like those we see around us: magnolia, laurel, dogwood, rose, grape vine, oak, poplar, willow, birch, and so on.

The other animals that lived on land with the dinosaurs were generally small. There were various kinds of lizards and later some snakes. There were tortoises, turtles and crocodiles too. At first, the skies would have contained only smallish pterosaurs – the gliding and flying reptiles. At the end of the Jurassic Period, the first birds came on the scene. By the end of the Cretaceous, there were some familiar birds like waders, divers, cormorants and owls. There were also some very large pterosaurs that looked like medium-sized leathery aeroplanes. In some places, you might have seen furry animals that seemed like shrews, rats or small cats.

On the next few pages some pictures of dinosaurs in their *habitats* are given. These show the dinosaurs that lived at different times, and also the other animals and plants that lived with them.

Upper Triassic - Lower Jurassic

This scene in southern Germany about 210 million years ago, shows some of the earliest dinosaurs. On the far side of the lake are two PLATEOSAURUS which may have eaten plants or meat. Two primitive crocodiles *(Protosuchus)* are just in front of them.

The flying reptile is *Kuehneosaurus* which could glide from branches in search of insects to eat. The wings were formed from flaps of skin that covered its extra long ribs. On the rock is an early lizard-like animal called *Glevosaurus* which probably ate

insects and grubs. In front of the rocks are two PROCOMPSOGNATHUS, small early meat-eaters. *Procompsognathus* was probably quick enough to catch lizards and early mammals, such as those in the bottom corner of this picture.

Middle Jurassic

By the Middle Jurassic, several important lines of dinosaurs had evolved. This scene is based on information from the area of Oxford, southern England. The best-known dinosaur is MEGALO-SAURUS, shown here looking hungrily at an early stegosaur, DACENTRURUS. In the background, a large sauropod, CETIO-SAURUS is looking for suitable plants to eat. These Middle Jurassic dinosaurs lived with more familiar-looking animals,

such as crocodiles, lizards and small mammals. However, in the skies we see some pterosaurs (*Rhamphocephalus*). The pterosaurs lived at the same time as the dinosaurs, and they may have fed on insects or dived for fish.

Upper Jurassic

Many remains have been found of dinosaurs that lived during the Upper Jurassic. This scene is based on information from the Morrison Formation of the western United States (Colorado, Wyoming, Utah), an area rich in fossils. On the banks of the river we can see some familiar long-necked sauropods such as DIPLODOCUS, BRACHIOSAURUS, and APATOSAURUS in the foreground. STEGOSAURUS, with its remarkable plates and spines, is shown at the water's edge. The small running dinosaur just beyond it is ORNITHOLESTES which probably fed on lizards

and mammals. The largest meat-eater of these times was ALLOSAURUS, shown here on the left in the front of the picture. At his feet are a colourful lizard and a cat-sized mammal. The large dinosaurs of the Morrison Formation lived in a land of lush vegetation and subtropical trees.

Lower Cretaceous

In the Lower Cretaceous, the *ornithopod* dinosaurs became important plant eaters. This scene, based on information from the Isle of Wight, southern England, shows the well-known IGUANODON feeding from a tall tree. *Iguanodon* is known from many specimens as the most common dinosaur at the time. The spikes on its thumb were used to help defend it from meat-eaters like the MEGALOSAURUS shown in this picture. Another ornithopod was HYPSILOPHODON. There are two specimens shown on the left of

this picture. The large *sauropods* were not common: we can see two PELOROSAURUS across the river. At the same time as these dinosaurs there were tortoises and crocodiles. The plants were subtropical and included ferns, palms and cycads.

Upper Cretaceous

Many different dinosaurs from the Upper Cretaceous have been discovered. This scene in southern Alberta, Canada about 70 million years ago shows a few well-known forms. On the left is the horn-faced TRICERATOPS, a large plant-eater. On the right are two *duck-billed* dinosaurs,

PARASAUROLOPHUS. These had extraordinary crests on their heads, like long tubes. In the middle, on the other side of the river, we can see two CORYTHOSAURUS, which were duckbills with a different kind of crest. The ostrich-like animal in the front is STENONYCHOSAURUS, a clever, agile meat eater. *Stenonychosaurus* is about to pounce on a frog. Several birds and a large pterosaur fly overhead. In the Upper Cretaceous there were many modern plants and animals such as lizards, mammals, frogs, various birds, and flowering plants like the rose.

Important Dinosaur Sites

Dinosaurs have been found on all continents except for Antarctica. (Fossil reptiles have been found on Antarctica, but these do not include dinosaurs.) A map of the world with the continents in their

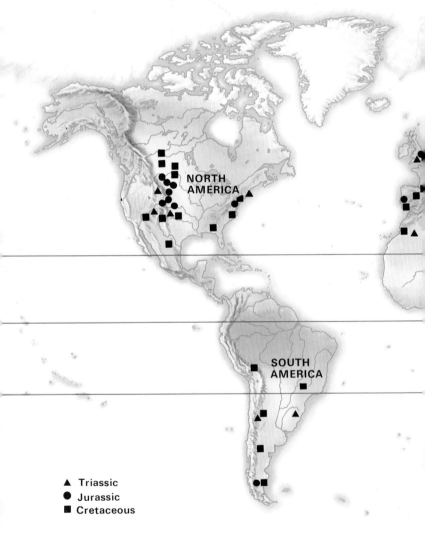

▲ Triassic
● Jurassic
■ Cretaceous

present arrangement shows that there are important dinosaur sites everywhere. The position of the sites depends on the age of the rocks, the habitats preserved, and a lucky discovery by a fossil collector. New dinosaur sites are discovered every year, and there are clearly many more to be found. If you turn back to page 20 you will see how the continents were arranged at the time of the dinosaurs.

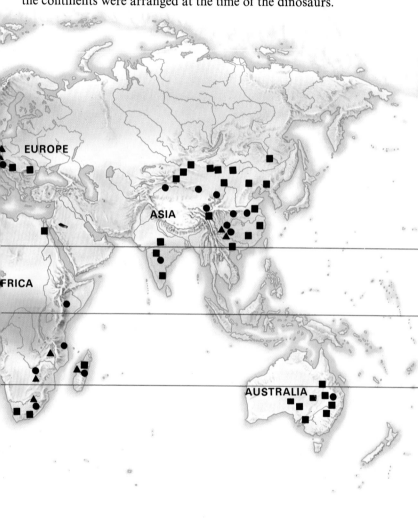

Dinosaur Dictionary

Many of the dinosaurs included in this dictionary have long, difficult names. The captions that open each dinosaur entry tell you how each name is pronounced and what it means. The captions also tell you to which order and suborder the dinosaur belongs, when it lived, and where remains have been found.

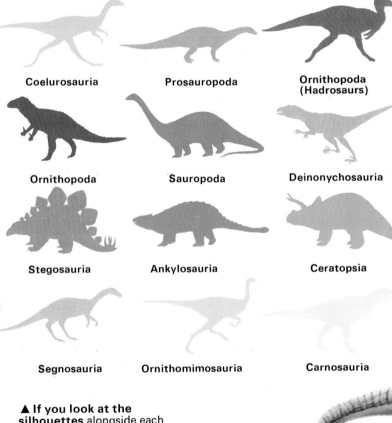

Coelurosauria

Prosauropoda

Ornithopoda
(Hadrosaurs)

Ornithopoda

Sauropoda

Deinonychosauria

Stegosauria

Ankylosauria

Ceratopsia

Segnosauria

Ornithomimosauria

Carnosauria

▲ **If you look at the silhouettes** alongside each dinosaur entry you will be able to tell at a glance to which group the dinosaur belonged. The figure beneath tells you how large the dinosaur was.

Acanthopholis

a-KAN-tho-FOLE-is
Spine bearer
Ornithischia: Ankylosauria
Middle to late Cretaceous
Southern England

Acrocanthosaurus

AK-ro-KANTH-oh-SAW-rus
Very spiny reptile
Saurischia; Carnosauria
Early Cretaceous
Oklahoma, USA

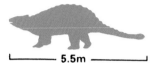

L_____ 5.5m _____J

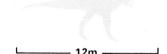

L_____ 12m _____J

Acanthopholis was a 5.5-metre-long animal with an armour of rows of oval plates made from bone set in the skin, and sharp spikes along the middle of its back. The best skeleton was found over a hundred years ago at Folkestone, southern England, in the chalk rocks at the very edge of the sea.

Acrocanthosaurus was a very large and terrifying meat-eater, about 12 metres long. It had 30-centimetre-long spines on its backbone. These suggest that it may have had a raised ridge or small sail along its back, similar to that of SPINOSAURUS. Several skeletons of this animal were found around 1950.

Acanthopholis

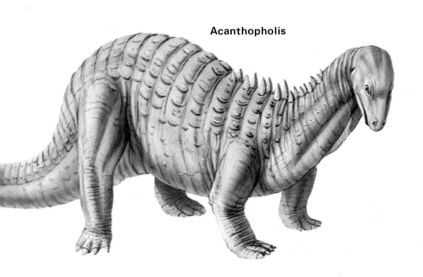

35

Alamosaurus

AL-am-oh-SAW-rus
Alamo reptile
Saurischia; Sauropoda
Late Cretaceous
Montana, New Mexico, Texas and
Utah, USA

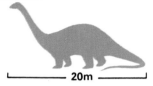

L———— 20m ————

Albertosaurus

al-BERT-oh-SAW-rus
Alberta reptile
Saurischia: Carnosauria
Alberta, Canada and Montana,
USA

Albertosaurus (sometimes called *Gorgosaurus*) also lived right at the end of the age of the dinosaurs. It was smaller than TYRANNOSAURUS at about 8 metres long, but it was still a fearsome beast. Dozens of bones and skeletons of *Albertosaurus* have been collected over the past hundred years, and these have been given different names. Recently palaeontologists have decided that they belong to the same animal.

Alamosaurus was the last sauropod dinosaur which lived right at the end of the age of the dinosaurs. It was named after the Alamo, a fort in San Antonio, Texas, which was the site of a famous siege last century. *Alamosaurus* was over 20 metres long. It has been unearthed and identified in many places in the western United States by its characteristic teeth.

L———— 8m ————

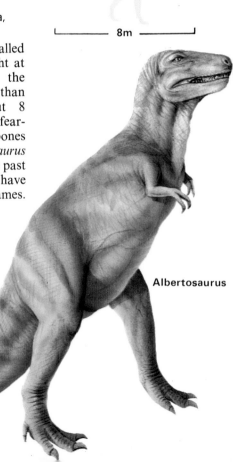

Albertosaurus

Allosaurus

AL-oh-SAW-rus
Foreign reptile
Saurischia: Carnosauria
Late Jurassic
USA and Tanzania

|———— **11m** ————|

Allosaurus was the main meat-eating dinosaur of the late Jurassic of North America, and it may have fed on well-known dinosaurs like APATOSAURUS, STEGOSAURUS and DRYOSAURUS. *Apatosaurus* was probably too big for *Allosaurus* to kill, but it may have fed on dead bodies. A skeleton of *Apatosaurus* has been found with *Allosaurus* tooth marks on some tail bones. *Allosaurus* was different from other meat-eating dinosaurs in the shape of its skull. It had a ridge along the top that ran from between the eyes to the tip of the snout. There were also some bumps above the eyes.

Allosaurus

37

Ammosaurus

AM-oh-SAW-rus
Sand reptile
Saurischia: Prosauropoda
Late Triassic/early Jurassic
Connecticut and Arizona, USA

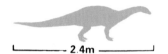

L———— 2.4m ————⌐

Ammosaurus was a 2.4-metre-long animal that could probably walk on all fours or on its hind legs. It is known from only a few partial skeletons. The first specimen was taken from a quarry in Connecticut a hundred years ago, at the time when a bridge was being built. This bridge was recently knocked down, and more of the same skeleton was found in the rubble.

Anatosaurus

an-AT-oh-SAW-rus
Duck reptile
Ornithischia: Ornithopoda
Late Cretaceous
Alberta, Canada

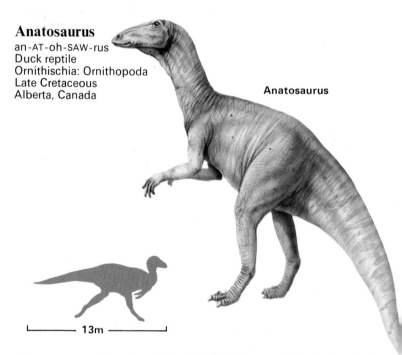

Anatosaurus

L——————— 13m ———————⌐

Anatosaurus was the classic 'duck-billed' dinosaur. It had a low skull, without a crest, and a broad snout area like a duck's beak. It was a large animal, up to 13 metres long. *Anatosaurus* is known by many skeletons, and some have been 'mummified' so that parts of the skin and other soft parts have been preserved (SEE page 162). There were several species of *Anatosaurus* that lived right through to the end of the Cretaceous period.

Anchiceratops

AN-ki-SER-a-tops
Close-horned face
Ornithischia: Ceratopsia
Late Cretaceous
Alberta, Canada

Anchiceratops skull

|_____ 6m _____|

Anchiceratops was 5–6 metres long. It had long horns above its eyes, but a short nose horn. It had a long neck-frill with knobs and spines pointing backwards. The horns, spines and frills were used for defence against meat-eaters. The particular pattern in *Anchiceratops* is different from all other ceratopsians, and may have helped the animals themselves to recognize other members of their own species.

Anchisaurus

AN-ki-SAW-rus
Close reptile
Saurischia: Prosauropoda
Late Triassic/early Jurassic
Connecticut, USA and South
Africa

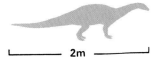

|_____ 2m _____|

Anchisaurus

Anchisaurus was a small lightly built animal, about 2 metres long. It had blunt diamond-shaped teeth spaced out along its jaw, and could have eaten plants or meat. *Anchisaurus* had strong limbs and large strong claws on its thumbs which it could have used to pull leaves from trees or to tear up flesh. The first dinosaur remains to be found in North America were collected in the late 18th century, and these included some bones of *Anchisaurus*.

39

ANKYLOSAURIA

an-KY-low-SAW-ree-a
Stiff reptiles
Ornithischia
Middle Jurassic to late
Cretaceous
Europe, North America, Asia

The Suborder Ankylosauria is known only from rare fossils in Jurassic rocks. However, a great variety of ankylosaurs occurred in the Cretaceous, and especially later on. They were all plant-eaters, and they had an armour of spines, knobs and spikes on their backs. There were two groups of ankylosaurs, some with narrow heads and no tail-clubs (the nodosaurids), and some with broad heads and heavy clubs at the ends of their tails (ankylosaurids).

Family Nodosauridae
>ACANTHOPHOLIS,
>HYLAEOSAURUS,
>NODOSAURUS,
>PANOPLOSAURUS,
>SILVISAURUS,
>STRUTHIOSAURUS

Family Ankylosauridae
>ANKYLOSAURUS,
>DYOPLOSAURUS,
>PINACOSAURUS

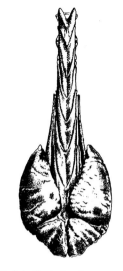

▲ **The tail club of Ankylosaurus:** a heavy knob formed from fused bone. Ankylosaurus could have swung the club from side to side with great force to knock and batter an attacker.

Ankylosaurus

an-KY-low-SAW-rus
Stiff reptile
Ornithischia: Ankylosauria
Late Cretaceous
Alberta, Canada and Montana,
USA

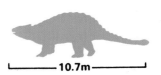

|——— 10.7m ———|

Ankylosaurus was the largest ankylosaur. It was over 10 metres long, and had the size and shape of a military tank. The body and limbs were powerful and protected by spines and bone plates. The tail was long and carried a heavy mass of bone at the end. An armour of heavy bone plates and horns even covered the top of the skull.

Antarctosaurus

an-TARCT-oh-SAW-rus
Southern reptile
Saurischia: Sauropoda
Late Cretaceous
South America and Asia

|——— 18m ———|

Antarctosaurus was probably one of the largest sauropods: its thigh bone alone was 2.3 metres long, which is taller than the front door of your house. Its head was really very small though – only 60 centimetres long and with weak peg-like teeth. *Antarctosaurus* is known only from partial skeletons and single bones from many different countries in South America and also in Asia.

Ankylosaurus

41

Apatosaurus

a-PAT-oh-SAW-rus
Headless reptile
Saurischia: Sauropoda
Late Jurassic
Colorado, Oklahoma, Utah and
Wyoming, USA

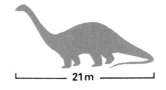

21m

Apatosaurus is one of the best known dinosaurs. It has been called *Brontosaurus* ('thunder reptile'), but the name *Apatosaurus* was given first. This was one of the giant dinosaurs collected in the 'bone wars' in the American West at the end of the 19th century by Othniel C. Marsh. *Apatosaurus* had a heavy body and heavy legs, a long neck and a long tail. You can see that it is heavier than DIPLODOCUS and not as tall as BRACHIOSAURUS, two of the other well-known sauropods. Until recently, *Apatosaurus* was thought to be most like CAMARASAURUS.

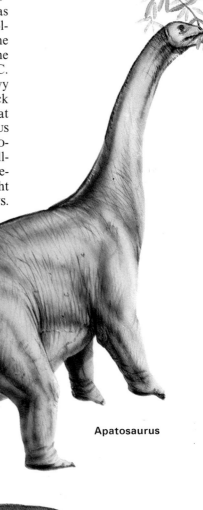

Apatosaurus

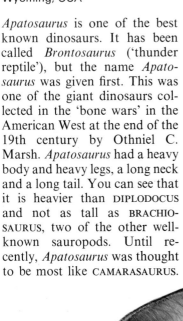

Skeletons of *Apatosaurus* had been found without their heads and they were reconstructed with a short skull, but this was shown to be wrong in 1979. Two dinosaur experts studied the notebooks made by the bone collectors a hundred years ago, and used these and other evidence to show that *Apatosaurus* had a long skull like *Diplodocus*.

Avimimus

av-i-MIME-us
Bird mimic
Saurischia: Ornithomimosauria
Late Cretaceous
Southern Mongolia

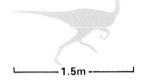

L——— 1.5m ———⌐

Avimimus was a small dinosaur, only 1–1.5 metres long, and very lightly built. Its legs are best known, and they show lots of bird-like features. In fact, the Russian scientist who described *Avimimus* in 1981 thought it was closely related to the birds. *Avimimus* had long slender legs, large eyes and a large brain.

Bagaceratops

BAG-a-SER-a-tops
Small horned face
Ornithischia: Ceratopsia
Late Cretaceous
Mongolia

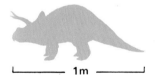

L——— 1m ———⌐

Bagaceratops was a very small ceratopsian – only 1 metre long. It had only a small neck frill, and a small horn on its snout. *Bagaceratops* had no teeth at the front of its mouth, but it had a tough 'beak' with which it could have nipped off branches and leaves.

Barapasaurus

ba-RA-pa-SAW-rus
Big-leg reptile
Saurischia: Sauropoda
Early Jurassic
Central India

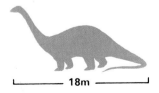

L——— 18m ———⌐

Barapasaurus is one of the oldest known sauropods. Its bones were found scattered like huge boulders across a wide area in fields in central India. When a huge bone was taken away in a truck, the driver said it was a big leg in the local dialect, and this is the origin of the name. The backbone shows special features, and the closest relatives of *Barapasaurus* are not known.

Barosaurus

BAR-o-SAW-rus
Heavy reptile
Saurischia: Sauropoda
Late Jurassic
South Dakota and Wyoming,
USA, and Tanzania

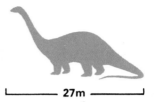

|———— 27m ————|

Barosaurus was a very long and rather slender sauropod, like DIPLODOCUS. The bones in its neck were each about 1 metre long. *Barosaurus* is a very important dinosaur, because it has been found in the western United States and in Tanzania, east Africa in rocks of the same age. This proves that the huge dinosaur could travel between the two areas and that they were joined together by land. It has been suggested that *Barosaurus*, and other large sauropods, used their long necks to feed high in the trees, just as giraffes do today. However, when *Barosaurus* lifted its head, the blood would have stopped flowing all the way up to its head. It probably only lifted its head up for short times.

Barosaurus

44

Brachiosaurus

BRACK-ee-oh-SAW-rus
Arm reptile
Saurischia: Sauropoda
Late Jurassic
Colorado, USA and Tanzania

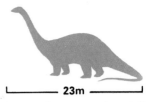

23m

Brachiosaurus is the tallest dinosaur known from complete skeletons. It had very long front legs, and if it stretched its neck upwards it could have looked over the roof of a three-storey building. The best skeletons were collected earlier this century in Tanzania. Hundreds of local workmen dug the bones up by hand and carried them to the port to be shipped to Germany. One huge skeleton of *Brachiosaurus* stands in the Humboldt Museum in East Berlin (SEE page 173). Brachiosaurus has its nostrils on top of its head, and it was once thought this was so that it could breathe under deep water. However, this is not likely because the water pressure would have stopped it from breathing.

Brachiosaurus

Brachyceratops

BRACK-ee-SER-a-tops
Short-horned face
Ornithischia: Ceratopsia
Late Cretaceous
Montana, USA and Alberta,
Canada

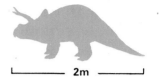

2m

Brachyceratops was a very small ceratopsian, only 2 metres long. It had a well developed slightly curved horn on its snout and smaller ones above its eyes. The frill was short. *Brachyceratops* is known from five or six skeletons, all of which are young animals. It is very likely that it was a young MONOCLONIUS, but this is hard to prove.

Brachylophosaurus

BRACK-ee-LOAF-oh-SAW-rus
Short-crested reptile
Ornithischia: Ornithopoda
Late Cretaceous
Alberta, Canada

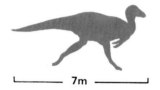

7m

Brachylophosaurus was one of the most primitive duck-billed dinosaurs, or hadrosaurs. It had a simple crest made from the nasal bones. These ran back between the eyes to form a broad plate. There was a little spike pointing backwards. The crest was solid in *Brachylophosaurus*, and its exact purpose is hard to decide. It may have been a kind of identification signal to let other dinosaurs know what kind of dinosaur it was.

Brontosaurus

(see APATOSAURUS)

Camarasaurus

kam-AR-a-SAW-rus
Chambered reptile
Saurischia: Sauropoda
Late Jurassic
Colorado, Oklahoma, Utah and
Wyoming, USA

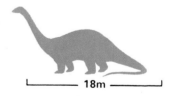

18m

Camarasaurus was a heavily built sauropod with a shorter tail and neck than APATOSAURUS or DIPLODOCUS. Its head was short and it had a blunt snout. Its nostrils were on top of its head and this has led people to suggest that it could have lived in water. Its whole body and head could have been submerged with just the nostrils showing.

Camarasaurus had long blunt teeth which pointed forwards. *Camarasaurus* probably used these to seize large mouthfuls of soft plants and leaves. Baby *Camarasaurus* specimens have been found in Utah and these show how the shape of the dinosaur changed as it grew up. The babies had relatively short necks and big heads, the body is heavy and the tail is short. The name *Camarasaurus* refers to the backbone, which had hollow areas or 'chambers'. (SEE ALSO page 9).

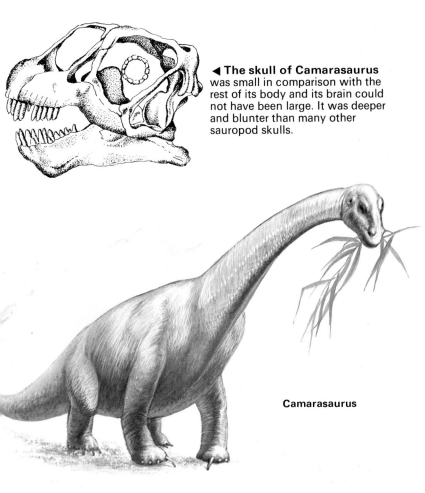

◀ **The skull of Camarasaurus** was small in comparison with the rest of its body and its brain could not have been large. It was deeper and blunter than many other sauropod skulls.

Camarasaurus

Camptosaurus

KAMP-toe-SAW-rus
Flexible reptile
Ornithischia: Ornithopoda
Late Jurassic and early
Cretaceous
Western Europe and western USA

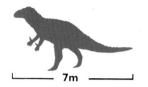

7m

Camptosaurus was heavily built and up to 7 metres long. It was similar in many respects to IGUANODON. *Camptosaurus* had long powerful hind-legs and much shorter arms. However, it had small hooves on each finger of the hand, which shows that it walked on all fours at least some of the time. About ten species of *Camptosaurus* have been described from different parts of Europe and North America. These all differ by size and proportions, but show how widespread this one dinosaur was.

Camptosaurus

Carcharodontosaurus

kar-KAR-oh-DONT-oh-SAW-rus
Carcharodon (a giant shark)
reptile
Saurischia: Carnosauria
Early Cretaceous
North Africa

├─────── 8m ───────┤

Carcharodontosaurus was a giant 8-metres-long meat-eater. It is known from incomplete remains found in the Sahara area. These include giant sharp teeth, 13–14 centimetres long. However, the fossils are not good enough to reconstruct the whole animal. It may have fed on plant-eaters that lived in the same area, like OURANOSAURUS.

CARNOSAURIA

KAR-no-SAW-ree-a
Meat-eating reptiles
Saurischia
Early Jurassic to late Cretaceous
Worldwide

The Infraorder Carnosauria includes all the giant meat-eating dinosaurs. There were three main families of carnosaurs: the megalosaurids, the spinosaurids (with spines on their backs), and the tyrannosaurids (with massive heads and tiny arms):

Family Megalosauridae
ALLOSAURUS,
CARCHARODONTOSAURUS,
CERATOSAURUS,
DILOPHOSAURUS,
DRYPTOSAURUS,
MEGALOSAURUS

Family Spinosauridae
ACROCANTHOSAURUS,
SPINOSAURUS

Family Tyrannosauridae
ALBERTOSAURUS, DASPLETO-
SAURUS, TARBOSAURUS,
TYRANNOSAURUS

CERATOPSIA

SER-a-TOP-see-a
Horn-faced reptiles
Ornithischia
Mid to late Cretaceous
North America, Asia

The Infraorder Ceratopsia includes the horned dinosaurs. They had horns on their noses and above their eyes, and a bony frill running back from the head over the neck. There were many different kinds, but they have only been found in North America and Asia. There were two primitive groups (psittacosaurids and protoceratopsids) and a large advanced group (ceratopsids).

Family Psittacosauridae
    PSITTACOSAURUS
Family Protoceratopsidae
    BAGACERATOPS,
    LEPTOCERATOPS,
    MICROCERATOPS,
    PROTOCERATOPS
Family Ceratopsidae
    ANCHICERATOPS,
    BRACHYCERATOPS,

Ceratosaurus

SER-a-toe-SAW-rus
Horned reptile
Saurischia: Carnosauria
Late Jurassic
Colorado, Oklahoma and Utah,
USA and Tanzania

L———— 6m ————J

Ceratosaurus was one of the most unusual meat-eating dinosaurs. It was quite large: up to 6 metres long, and it had typical massive sharp fangs. However, it had a horn on its nose. This was probably not to protect itself; it may have been used by males in fighting for a mate.

Ceratosaurus

CHASMOSAURUS,
MONOCLONIUS,
PACHYRHINOSAURUS,
PENTACERATOPS,
STYRACOSAURUS,
TOROSAURUS, TRICERATOPS

Cetiosaurus

SEET-ee-oh-SAW-rus
Whale reptile
Saurischia: Sauropoda
Middle to late Jurassic
England and North Africa

18m

Cetiosaurus was one of the earliest dinosaurs to be discovered. It was named in 1841 from odd teeth and bones, and a partial skeleton was found in 1870 near Oxford. A thigh bone found in Morocco in 1979 was 2 metres long: the height of a tall man. *Cetiosaurus* was one of the earliest sauropods and

it was primitive in some respects. For example, its massive backbone was solid. Later sauropods had hollow areas in their bones to cut down the weight.

Cetiosaurus

Chasmosaurus

KAZ-mo-SAW-rus
Gape reptile
Ornithischia: Ceratopsia
Late Cretaceous
Alberta, Canada and New Mexico,
USA

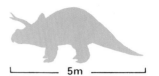

5m

Chasmosaurus was the earliest long-frilled ceratopsian. At the back of the head there is a long frill made from the skull bones which have grown backwards. The frill is longer than the skull itself, and it has large holes in it to make it weigh less. The frill covered the back of the neck which could have been a soft place for TYRANNOSAURUS to bite into. The strong neck muscles that *Chasmosaurus* needed to hold up its heavy head would have been fixed to the frill. There were small horns over the eyes and one on the nose. *Chasmosaurus* was over 5 metres long (SEE ALSO page 164).

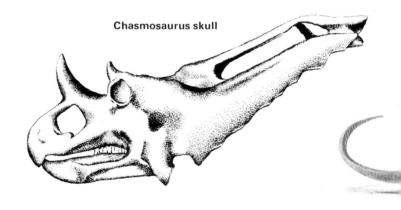

Chasmosaurus skull

Claosaurus

CLAY-oh-SAW-rus
Branched reptile
Ornithischia: Ornithopoda
Late Cretaceous
Kansas, USA

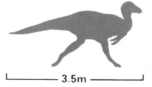

3.5m

Claosaurus was one of the earliest duck-billed dinosaurs. The duck bills, like CORYTHOSAURUS, PARASAUROLOPHUS and TSINTAOSAURUS, often had fancy crests on top of their heads. *Claosaurus* hardly had any crest at all. It was primitive in some other features of its legs and feet. *Claosaurus* had a slim body and it was only 3.5 metres or so long.

Coelophysis

SEEL-oh-FY-sis
Hollow form
Saurischia: Coelurosauria
Late Triassic
New Mexico and Massachusetts, USA

3m

Coelophysis

Coelophysis is the oldest dinosaur that we know well. There are several late Triassic dinosaurs of about the same age – such as ISCHISAURUS, PROCOMPSOGNATHUS, SALTOPUS, and STAURIKOSAURUS – but each of these is known from only one or two skeletons. In 1947, a mass of a hundred or more specimens was found at Ghost Ranch, New Mexico. The specimens of *Coelophysis* dug up there included young and old animals which ranged in size from 1–3 metres long. *Coelophysis* was very slim and it could have run on two legs or on four. The neck and tail were long. The hands had only three fingers, but they were strong. *Coelophysis* had a long narrow head, and its sharp jagged teeth show that it ate meat – probably the small lizard-like animals that are found with it. Some of the skeletons were found with small *Coelophysis* bones inside. It was thought that these were babies, ready to be born. However, they are rather too big for that, and it may be that *Coelophysis* was a cannibal.

53

COELUROSAURIA

seel-OO-roe-SAW-ree-a
Hollow reptiles
Saurischia
Late Triassic to late Cretaceous
Worldwide

The Infraorder Coelurosauria includes a variety of small and medium-sized meat-eating dinosaurs. Most of them ran upright on their hind legs. There are two main groups which can be told apart mainly by the shape of the head and hands. The coelophysids (late Triassic) had large wedge-shaped heads and three or four claws on their hands. The coelurids (late Jurassic) had small low heads and always three claws on their hands.

Family Coelophysidae
COELOPHYSIS,
HALTICOSAURUS,
PROCOMPSOGNATHUS,
SALTOPUS, ?SEGISAURUS,
SYNTARSUS
Family Coeluridae
COELURUS,
COMPSOGNATHUS,
ORNITHOLESTES

Coelurus

seel-OO-rus
Hollow tail
Saurischia: Coelurosauria
Late Jurassic
Wyoming, USA

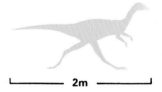

2m

Coelurus was a very small dinosaur – only 2 metres long and very lightly built. Its skull would have fitted in a man's hand. Its bones were very light: the tail vertebrae were hollow. The hand had only three fingers: the thumb was short and the other two fingers very long with sharp curved claws. *Coelurus* was very like ORNITHOLESTES.

Compsognathus

KOMP-SOW-NAY-thus
Pretty jaw
Saurischia: Coelurosauria
Late Jurassic
Southern Germany and France

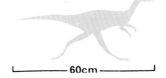

|— 60cm —|

Compsognathus was closely related to COELURUS, and lived at about the same time, but in Europe. The adult was one of the smallest known dinosaurs. *Compsognathus* was no bigger than a hen. A single beautiful skeleton was found in Germany in 1861. In this specimen, the tail is lifted up, and the head is bent back over the tail. This was thought to be an unnatural position showing that *Compsognathus* was in agony. However, in many dead animals, the head bends back as the neck muscles dry out. This specimen, like some of those of COELOPHYSIS, had small bones inside it, and it was thought that *Compsognathus* was also a cannibal. However, the bones now turn out to have belonged to a lizard.

A herd of Compsognathus

Corythosaurus

ko-RITH-oh-SAW-rus
Helmeted reptile
Ornithischia: Ornithopoda
Late Cretaceous
Alberta, Canada

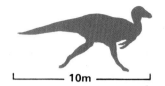

— 10m —

Corythosaurus is one of the best known of the hadrosaurs (duck-billed dinosaurs). It was a large animal – over 10 metres long. The crest on top of the head was high and narrow from side to side. It was shaped like half a dinner plate set up on edge. The nasal tubes ran from the nostrils on the snout up into the crest and then down again into the mouth. *Corythosaurus* may have used this complicated breathing tube system to make loud bellows and honks. There are several species of *Corythosaurus* which are based on the shape of the crest. The closest relative of *Corythosaurus* was LAMBEOSAURUS.

Corythosaurus

Dacentrurus

DA-sen-TROO-rus
Pointed tail
Ornithischia: Stegosauria
Middle to late Jurassic
Western Europe

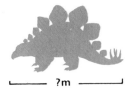

L——— ?m ———⌐

Dacentrurus was one of the earliest stegosaurs. It is only known from odd bones found in England, France and Portugal, so a restoration cannot be given. *Dacentrurus* had paired spines on its back, but probably no plates. Some of the specimens show close similarities with STEGOSAURUS.

Daspletosaurus

da-SPLEET-oh-SAW-rus
Frightful reptile
Saurischia: Carnosauria
Late Cretaceous
Alberta, Canada

L——— 8.5m ———⌐

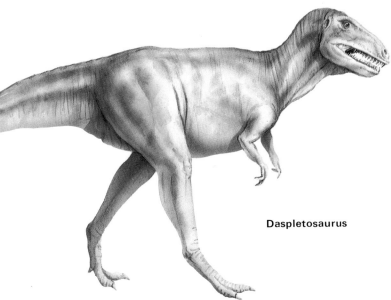

Daspletosaurus

Daspletosaurus was a fearsome huge 8.5-metre-long meat-eater. It had a huge head, deep jaws and dagger-like teeth. It had powerful hind legs, each with three toes, but the arms were weak and only had two fingers each. *Daspletosaurus* could have attacked and eaten the duck-billed dinosaurs or ceratopsians that lived with it.

57

Deinocheirus

DINE-oh-KIRE-us
Terrible hand
Saurischia: Deinonychosauria
Late Cretaceous
Southern Mongolia

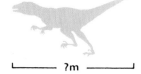

L——— ?m ———J

Deinocheirus is one of the most amazing dinosaur fossils known. It is a pair of huge arms and nothing else. Each arm was 2.6 metres long. Each hand had only three fingers, and these all had powerful claws. The claws themselves were each about 25 centimetres long, the size of a butcher's heavy chopping knife. If the arms belonged to a meat-eating dinosaur of a normal shape, it would have been unbelievably huge. We cannot even guess what the whole animal looked like.

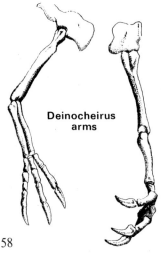

**Deinocheirus
arms**

DEINONYCHOSAURIA

DIE-no-NIKE-oh-SAW-ree-a
Saurischia
Cretaceous
North America and Asia

The Infraorder Deinonychosauria contains some of the most remarkable and fearsome meat-eating dinosaurs. There were three groups of the deinonychosaurs.

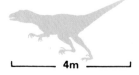

Family Dromaeosauridae
DEINONYCHUS,
DROMAEOSAURUS,
?ITEMIRUS, ?NOASAURUS,
VELOCIRAPTOR
Family Saurornithoididae
SAURORNITHOIDES,
STENONYCHOSAURUS
Family Deinocheiridae
DEINOCHEIRUS,
?THERIZINOSAURUS

Deinonychus

DIE-no-NIKE-us
Terrible claw
Saurischia: ?Deinonychosauria
Early Cretaceous
Western USA

L——— 4m ———J

Deinonychus was one of the most exciting dinosaurs discovered in the 1960s. It was represented by well preserved skeletons and these allowed detailed restorations. *Deinonychus* was 3–4 metres long, and was larger than its relatives. DROMAEOSAURUS and VELOCIRAPTOR. *Deinonychus* had strong grasping fingers on its hands. Its most remarkable feature was the large curved scythe-like claw on the second toe of the foot. The other toes had shorter claws. When *Deinonychus* ran, it flicked the big claw back and

Deinonychus

Dicraeosaurus

die-KRAY-oh-SAW-rus
Forked reptile
Saurischia: Sauropoda
Late Jurassic

|— 20m —|

placed the shorter toes on the ground. *Deinonychus* used its big claw to attack other dinosaurs. It would have balanced on one foot in order to swing the claw to open the belly of its prey. Its tail was stiffened by long rods of bone.

Dicraeosaurus was related to APATOSAURUS and DIPLODOCUS. The name 'forked reptile' refers to a strange feature of the vertebrae of the backbone. The spine on top of each vertebrae split in two and formed a shape like a letter Y. The skull was long and sloping (compare it with the skull of CAMARASAURUS, which is short).

Dilophosaurus

die-LOAF-oh-SAW-rus
Two-ridged reptile
Saurischia: Carnosauria
Early Jurassic
Arizona

L———— 6m ————⅃

Dilophosaurus is the oldest well-known large meat-eating dinosaur. It is related to MEGALOSAURUS. The most amazing thing about *Dilophosaurus* is that it had two very thin ridges on top of its skull. These were shaped like a pair of half dinner plates set up on edge and side by side. *Dilophosaurus* had sharp fangs, and was 6 metres long.

Diplodocus

dip-LOD-oh-kus
Double beam
Saurischia: Sauropoda
Late Jurassic
Colorado, Montana, Utah and
Wyoming, USA

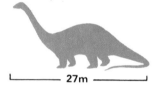

L——— 27m ————⅃

Diplodocus was 27 metres long. Most of this length was made up from the very long thin neck and long whip-like tail. The name 'double beam' described a special feature of the backbone. There were small bones below the backbone which had a piece running forwards as well as the normal piece that runs back – a 'double beam'. Many skeletons of *Diplodocus* were collected in the American West about 1900. The Scottish-American millionaire Andrew Carnegie paid for much of the collecting, and the best skeleton was called *Diplodocus carnegii*.

Diplodocus

61

Dravidosaurus

dra-VID-oh-SAW-rus
Reptile from southern India
Ornithischia: Stegosauria
Late Cretaceous
Southern India

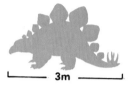

3m

Dravidosaurus is the last known stegosaur. Most stegosaurs, like STEGOSAURUS and KENTROSAURUS, come from the late Jurassic, so that there is a span of millions of years between these and *Dravidosaurus*. *Dravidosaurus* had an armour of plates on its back, and strange spines which bulged halfway up. It was named in 1979.

Dromaeosaurus

DROME-ee-oh-SAW-rus
Running reptile
Saurischia: Deinonychosauria
Late Cretaceous
Alberta, Canada

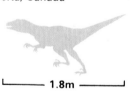

1.8m

Dromaeosaurus was a small active running dinosaur. It was very like DEINONYCHUS and had a special sharp claw on its foot for attacking other dinosaurs. *Dromaeosaurus* was smaller than *Deinonychus*: it was only 1.8 metres long, and it could have just looked a ten-year old child in the eye if it stood up straight. *Dromaeosaurus* was a fierce little meat-eater – it was intelligent and quick-moving, and may have eaten lizards, turtles and baby dinosaurs. It is only known from a skull and odd bones of the skeleton.

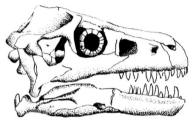

Dromaeosaurus skull

Dryosaurus

DRY-oh-SAW-rus
Oak reptile
Ornithischia: Ornithopoda
Late Jurassic
Western USA, Tanzania

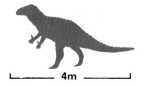

4m

Dryosaurus was a relative of HYPSILOPHODON, but much larger: *Dryosaurus* was 3–4 metres long. It had long powerful legs, and strong arms, each with five fingers. *Dryosaurus* could have run fast on its hind legs. Its tail was stiff and it could have been used for balance. *Dryosaurus* probably used its hands to gather plants to eat. It had sharp ridged cheek teeth, but not teeth at the front of the jaw. *Dryosaurus* is known from several skeletons and skulls from Africa and North America, which proves that these two parts of the world were in contact 140 million years ago. *Dryosaurus* lived with the well-known sauropods APATOSAURUS, BRACHIOSAURUS and DIPLODOCUS, the stegosaurs STEGOSAURUS and KENTROSAURUS, and the meat-eaters ALLOSAURUS, COELURUS and ELAPHROSAURUS.

Dryosaurus

Dryptosaurus

DRIP-toe-SAW-rus
Tearing reptile
Saurischia: Carnosauria
Late Cretaceous
USA

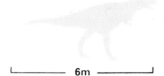

L—————— 6m ——————⌐

Dryptosaurus was a meat-eater that lived all over North America. Many finds of odd teeth and jaw bones have been named as *Dryptosaurus* – at least 12 species have been described, and yet no one really knows what it looked like. The only skeleton was collected in 1866 and named *Laelaps* by E. D. Cope, one of the famous dinosaur collectors of the North American 'bone wars'. The name *Laelaps* was based on a hunting dog from the ancient Greek myths, and Cope had a model made that showed *Laelaps* fiercely leaping through the air to attack another dinosaur. Unfortunately, we cannot use the name *Laelaps* because an insect had been given that name before.

Dyoplosaurus

die-0-plo-SAW-rus
Doubly armoured reptile
Ornithischia: Ankylosauria
Late Cretaceous
Alberta, Canada

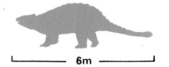

L————— 6m —————⌐

Dyoplosaurus was a large ankylosaur which was closely related to EUOPLOCEPHALUS. *Dyoplosaurus* had massive legs, and it was over 6 metres long. It was as big as a military tank and probably as heavy. *Dyoplosaurus* had a massive head which was 35 centimetres wide. The bones of the skull were heavily fused together, and there were extra bone plates on top. The end of the tail formed a club. The last ten bones of the tail were joined together by fused bone and strengthened tendons ⋅ along either side. At the very end was a great lump of bone made from four joined blocks. The whole solid club was 1.3 metres long and very heavy. It must have been a useful weapon against TYRANNOSAURUS.

Edmontosaurus

ed-MONT-oh-SAW-rus
Edmonton reptile
Ornithischia: Ornithopoda
Late Cretaceous
Alberta, Canada and Montana,
USA

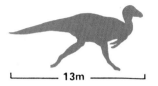

13m

Edmontosaurus was a flat-headed duck-billed dinosaur, rather like ANATOSAURUS and SHANTUNGOSAURUS. *Edmontosaurus* is quite well known because several skeletons have been found. It was one of the largest duck-bills, at about 13 metres long. The skull was low in front and high at the back. There was a wide duck-like beak (as in *Anatosaurus*). *Edmontosaurus* did not have a crest, unlike many duck-bills. *Edmontosaurus* had about a thousand strong teeth, and probably fed on tough plants which needed to be well chopped up before swallowing.

Edmontosaurus

Elaphrosaurus

ee-LAF-roe-SAW-rus
Light reptile
Saurischia: Ornithomimosauria
Late Jurassic
Tanzania

3.5m

Elaphrosaurus is the oldest known ornithomimosaur: all the others, like ORNITHOMIMUS and STRUTHIOMIMUS, lived in the late Cretaceous, 70 million years later. *Elaphrosaurus* was 3.5 metres long, and not as ostrich-like as its later relatives. It had long slender legs and was obviously a fast runner. Its arms were short. Both the feet and hands only had three fingers or toes. *Elaphrosaurus* is best known from the famous Tendaguru dinosaur beds in Tanzania. These have also yielded the dinosaurs BAROSAURUS, BRACHIOSAURUS and KENTROSAURUS.

Elaphrosaurus

Euhelopus

yoo-HEL-oh-pus
True marsh foot
Saurischia: Sauropoda
Early Cretaceous
Eastern China

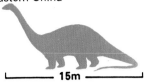

|— 15m —|

Euhelopus was a large sauropod related to CAMARASAURUS and OPISTHOCOELICAUDIA. It may have been 10–15 metres long. It had a very long neck and a rather long head. The front legs were longer than the hind legs, and the back sloped, as in *Camarasaurus*. This was one of the first dinosaurs from China to be described. It was collected in the 1920s by a Swedish expedition.

Euskelosaurus

YOOSK-el-oh-SAW-rus
True limbed reptile
Saurischia: Prosauropoda
Late Triassic/early Jurassic
South Africa

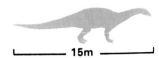

|— 15m —|

Euskelosaurus was one of the first dinosaurs to be described from Africa. A small set of leg bones was sent to England from South Africa and named *Euskelosaurus* in 1866. Since then, many more bones of this animal have been found. The bones are huge: the thigh bone was a metre long. Because of the poor fossils, it is not certain exactly what the relationships of *Euskelosaurus* were. It was a prosauropod, and it may have been related to either PLATEOSAURUS or MELANORO-SAURUS.

Fabrosaurus

FAB-roe-SAW-rus
Fabre's reptile
Ornithischia: Ornithopoda
Late Triassic/early Jurassic
Lesotho, South Africa

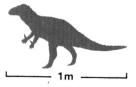

Fabrosaurus was an early primitive ornithopod related to SCUTELLOSAURUS. It was only 1 metre long and would not have been able to look over your dinner table at home if it had stood up as straight as it could. *Fabrosaurus*· was very lightly built and ran on its hind legs. It had strong arms and hands. The teeth were strong and they had frilled or knobbly edges. This shows that *Fabrosaurus* could use its teeth to chop up tough vegetation.

Fabrosaurus

Gallimimus

GAL-ih-MIME-us
Hen mimic
Saurischia: Ornithomimosauria
Late Cretaceous
Southern Mongolia

4m

Gallimimus

Gallimimus was probably the largest ornithomimosaur. It was about 4 metres long, slightly bigger than its close relatives ORNITHOMIMUS and STRUTHIOMIMUS. *Gallimimus* had hands that could not grasp things, and so probably could not have torn meat up. It has been suggested that it scraped at the soil and may have fed on eggs. *Gallimimus* had a long snout with a broad flat end.

Geranosaurus

jer-AN-oh-SAW-rus
Crane reptile
Ornithischia: Ornithopoda
Late Triassic / early Jurassic
South Africa

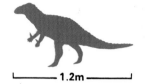

L—— 1.2m ——⌐

Geranosaurus was a small ornithopod that was closely related to HETERODONTOSAURUS and LYCORHINUS. It is only known from parts of its jaws and a few other bones. The jaws show that it had sharp teeth at the front of the jaw, a pair of fangs behind, and ridged cheek teeth at the back. The front teeth were used to snip off pieces of plants.

Hadrosaurus

HAD-roe-SAW-rus
Big reptile
Ornithischia: Ornithopoda
Late Cretaceous
New Jersey and New Mexico,
USA, and Alberta, Canada

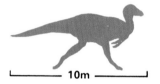

L—— 10m ——⌐

Hadrosaurus was the first dinosaur to be named from North America. A skeleton without the skull was collected from New Jersey and named *Hadrosaurus* in 1858. It had a long low skull with a typical 'duck-billed' shape, like ANATOSAURUS and EDMONTOSAURUS. There was a rounded hump in front of the eyes and above the nostrils.

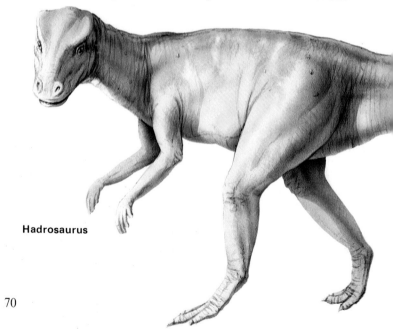

Hadrosaurus

70

Halticosaurus

hal-TIK-oh-SAW-rus
Nimble reptile
Saurischia: Coelurosauria
Late Triassic
Southern Germany

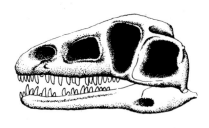

L————— 5.5m —————J

Halticosaurus skull

Halticosaurus was a large coelurosaur, up to 5.5 metres long. It had five fingers on its hand, a feature of primitive dinosaurs. The arms were short, and the legs were strong. The head was long and large. In the drawing of the skull you can see the pointed meat-eating teeth, and the light construction, with lots of holes. From the front, the holes are the nostril, an opening of unknown function, the eye socket, and jaw muscle openings. Two skeletons and a skull of *Halticosaurus* have been found in Germany together with the larger prosauropod PLATEOSAURUS.

Heterodontosaurus

HET-er-oh-DONT-oh-SAW-rus
Reptile with different teeth
Ornithischia: Ornithopoda
Late Triassic/early Jurassic
South Africa

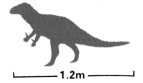

L————— 1.2m —————J

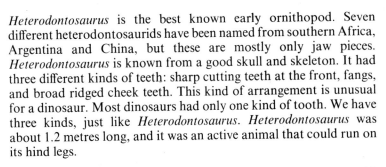

Heterodontosaurus is the best known early ornithopod. Seven different heterodontosaurids have been named from southern Africa, Argentina and China, but these are mostly only jaw pieces. *Heterodontosaurus* is known from a good skull and skeleton. It had three different kinds of teeth: sharp cutting teeth at the front, fangs, and broad ridged cheek teeth. This kind of arrangement is unusual for a dinosaur. Most dinosaurs had only one kind of tooth. We have three kinds, just like *Heterodontosaurus*. *Heterodontosaurus* was about 1.2 metres long, and it was an active animal that could run on its hind legs.

71

Homalocephale

hom-AL-oh-KEF-al-ee
Level head
Ornithischia: Pachycephalosauria
Late Cretaceous
Mongolia

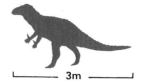

L—— 3m ——⌐

Homalocephale was a medium-sized pachycephalosaur with a flat head. The top of its skull was very thick and the surface was rough. It was covered with pits and bony knobs. The most important feature of *Homalocephale* is that the skeleton is well known. Many pachycephalosaurs are only known from the thickened skull roofs. In *Homalocephale* the hip bones are very wide and they are loosely attached to the backbone. It has been suggested that *Homalocephale* may have given birth to live young, rather than laying eggs.

Hylaeosaurus

HY-lee-oh-SAW-rus
Woodland reptile
Ornithischia: Ankylosauria
Early Cretaceous
Southern England

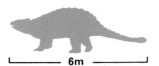

L———— 6m ————⌐

Hylaeosaurus is the oldest fairly well known ankylosaur. There are some partial skeletons, but its armour is more often found. The animal was about 6 metres long. It had an armour of spines that stuck out sideways and upwards along the back and tail. The top of the head was thick and bony. This was one of the first dinosaurs to be named. A skeleton

from Sussex, south-east England, was named as *Hylaeosaurus* in 1833.

Hypacrosaurus

hie-PAK-roe-SAW-rus
Below-the-top reptile
Ornithischia: Ornithopoda
Late Cretaceous
Alberta, Canada and Montana,
USA

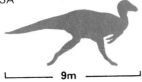

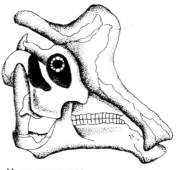

**Hypacrosaurus
skull**

Hypacrosaurus was a large duck-billed dinosaur, about 9 metres long. It was an advanced form, related to CORYTHOSAURUS and LAMBEOSAURUS. *Hypacrosaurus* had a short, high skull and its crest was rounded, but lower and fatter than that of *Corythosaurus*. The crest ran out back-wards into a solid bony spike. If you look at the drawing of the skull, you can see that the crest is built up from the bones at the front of the skull. These have grown up and backwards. *Hypacrosaurus* had dozens of strong teeth which formed a large area for grinding and chopping tough plant food. As the teeth wore down they were replaced by new ones.

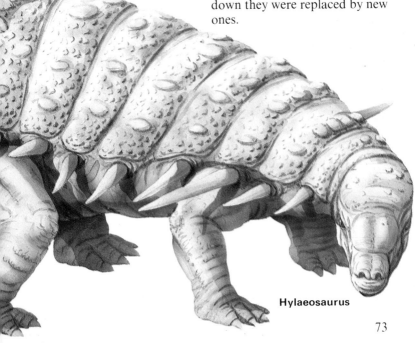

Hylaeosaurus

73

Hypselosaurus

HIP-sel-oh-SAW-rus
High-ridged reptile
Saurischia: Sauropoda
Late Cretaceous
France

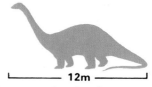

Hypselosaurus was a medium-sized sauropod related to ALAMO-SAURUS, SALTASAURUS and TITANOSAURUS. *Hypselosaurus* was about 12 metres long. It had a short head with small teeth, and a long tail. The most interesting thing about *Hypselosaurus* is that its bones have been found together with large eggs and pieces of egg shell in the south of France. The eggs were big – about 30 centimetres long and 25 centimetres across. More information about these eggs is given later in the book (SEE page 159).

Hypsilophodon

hip-see-LOAF-oh-don
High-ridged tooth
Ornithischia: Onithopoda
Early Cretaceous
Southern England

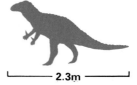

Hypsilophodon is an interesting medium-sized ornithopod. It was 1.4–2.3 metres long. It had short arms, each with five fingers, and long legs, each with four toes. *Hypsilophodon* could run fast, and it had a long stiff tail which it used for balance. It was once thought that *Hypsilophodon* climbed trees, but this is not likely since it could not grasp the branches. *Hypsilophodon* had no teeth at the front of its mouth, but only a bony 'beak', and a row of sharp chopping teeth further back. It could have nipped plants off with its beak, and chopped them up with its cheek teeth.

Hypsilophodon

Iguanodon

ig-WA-no-DON
Iguana tooth
Ornithischia: Ornithischia
Early Cretaceous
Western Europe, North Africa

Iguanodon

Iguanodon was the second dinosaur to be named – in 1825. *Iguanodon* was up to 9 metres long and stood 5 metres high – about the height of a double-decker bus. *Iguanodon* had strong hind limbs with three big toes, each with a hoof-like nail. The hand had four long fingers and a pointed spike-like thumb, which was probably used as a weapon. The tail was flattened and stiff, and *Iguanodon* could have run well on its hind legs or walked on all fours. There were no teeth at the front of the jaw – only a bony beak like that of HYPSILOPHODON. The cheek teeth were strong and ridged. *Iguanodon* may have pulled plants into its mouth with its tongue, and nipped them off with its beak.

9m

75

Ischisaurus

ISH-ih-SAW-rus
Ischigualasto (where found)
reptile
Saurischia:? Prosauropoda
Late Triassic
Argentina

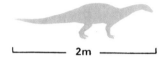

2m

Ischisaurus is one of the oldest known dinosaurs, and rather a poorly known animal. Only two specimens are known, and these include parts of the skull and legs. *Ischisaurus* was a medium-sized animal, 2 metres or so long. The arms were short and the hind legs rather longer, which suggests that *Ischisaurus* may have run on its hind legs.

Itemirus

EAT-em-EE-rus
Itemir (where found)
Saurischia: ? Deinonychosauria
Late Cretaceous
Central Asia

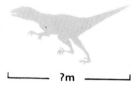

?m

Itemirus was a lightly built, agile meat-eating dinosaur. It is very poorly known, however. It was named from a braincase in 1976.

This is supposed to be like the braincase of DROMAEOSAURUS in parts and that of TYRANNO-SAURUS in other parts.

Kentrosaurus

KEN-tro-SAW-rus
Pointed reptile
Ornithischia: Stegosauria
Late Jurassic
Tanzania

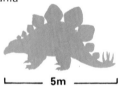

5m

Kentrosaurus was a large 5-metre-long plated dinosaur. Some good skeletons were collected at the famous Tendaguru site in Tanzania. It was rather like STEGOSAURUS which lived in North America at the same time, except that *Kentrosaurus* had more primitive armour like that of LEXOVISAURUS. *Kentrosaurus* had small triangular plates on the neck and shoulders, and long spines on the back and tail.

Kentrosaurus

Lambeosaurus

LAM-bee-oh-SAW-rus
Lambe's (Canadian palaeontologist) reptile
Ornithischia: Ornithopoda
Late Cretaceous
Alberta, Canada and Montana, USA

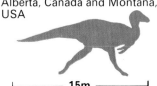

├─────── **15m** ───────┤

Lambeosaurus was a crested duck-billed dinosaur related to CORYTHOSAURUS and HYPACRO-SAURUS. *Lambeosaurus* had a square-shaped crest which poin-ted forwards, and with a long spine running backwards. The nostrils ran up from the snout and through the crest, so that the whole thing was hollow. In some specimens of *Lambeosaurus*, the crest is bigger than the skull.

Lambeosaurus was big – about 15 metres long – and its bones are massive.

Lambeosaurus

77

Leptoceratops

LEP-toe-SER-a-tops
Slim-horned face
Ornithischia: Ceratopsia
Late Cretaceous
Alberta, Canada, Wyoming, USA
and Mongolia

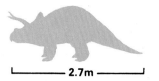

2.7m

Leptoceratops was a small horned dinosaur related to BAGACERATOPS and PROTOCERATOPS. It had short arms and long hind legs, so it probably ran upright. The skull was low and it had no trace of horns at all, unlike its relatives. *Leptoceratops* had a small frill at the back of its skull, and it is clearly a primitive form. *Leptoceratops* was 1.8–2.7 metres long.

Lexovisaurus

lex-OVE-ih-SAW-rus
Lexovi (ancient tribe) reptile
Ornithischia: Stegosauria
Middle Jurassic
England and France

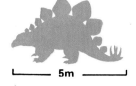

5m

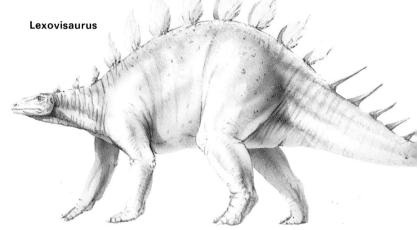

Lexovisaurus

Lexovisaurus is one of the oldest known stegosaurs. We know about it from pieces of armour and limb bones from England and northern France. The French specimens show that *Lexovisaurus* was probaly rather like KENTROSAURUS. Its armour was a selection of flat plates and round pointed spines that ran along the back and tail. There was a pair of very long spines over the hips. *Lexovisaurus* was probably about 5 metres long.

Lufengosaurus

loo-FENG-oh-SAW-rus
Lufeng reptile
Saurischia: Prosauropoda
Late Triassic /early Jurassic
Lufeng, southern China

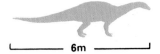

6m

Lufengosaurus is one of the oldest Chinese dinosaurs and it shows that there were pro-sauropods all over the world. It was closely related to PLATEO-SAURUS, and was quite large: it was about 6 metres long. *Lufengosaurus* had a long skull and its teeth were widely spaced. It had long powerful hind legs and shorter arms. *Lufengosaurus* could probably walk upright on its hind legs or on all fours. The diet of these plateosaurs is a mystery. It has usually been assumed that they ate plants, but the small, spaced teeth had fairly sharp edges and could have been used for eating meat also.

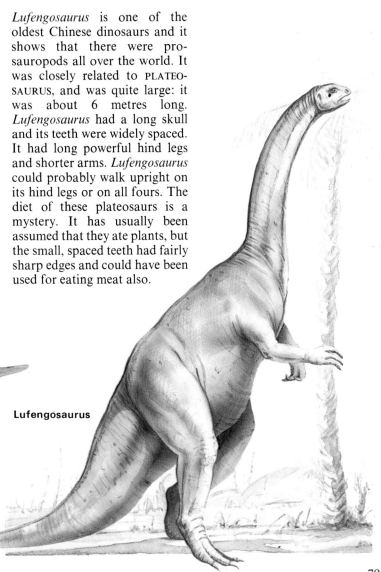

Lufengosaurus

79

Lycorhinus

LIE-koe-RINE-us
Wolf snout
Ornithischia: Ornithopoda
Late Triassic/early Jurassic
South Africa

Maiasaura and young

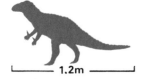

L———— 1.2m ————J

Lycorhinus is an important, but very poorly known, dinosaur. It was one of the early ornithopods – a heterodontosaurid – and its close relatives are GERANO-SAURUS and HETERODONTO-SAURUS. *Lycorhinus* was named in 1924 from a part of the left jaw of a very small dinosaur. It shows a large tusk, and teeth as in *Heterodontosaurus*.

Maiasaura

MY-a-SAW-ra
Good-mother reptile
Ornithischia: Ornithopoda
Late Cretaceous
Montana, USA

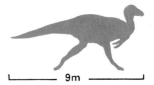

L———— 9m ————J

Maiasaura is one of the most important dinosaurs found recently. In 1978 and 1979, skeletons of adult *Maiasaura* were found with nests and babies. The mother was about 9 metres long, and the young animals only 1 metre long. The nests were made in mounds which were 3 metres across, and the eggs were arranged in several layers. In each layer the eggs, which were shaped like sausages, lay in circles like the spokes of a wheel. The mother *Maiasaura* clearly laid her eggs carefully, and must have arranged them in this regular pattern. She covered each layer with sand, and then covered the whole nest of eggs so that they were all kept warm until the young ones hatched out. However, the young animals that have been found were not hatchlings, so they were staying around the nest as they grew up. This has suggested that these dinosaurs looked after their young (SEE ALSO page 160).

Mamenchisaurus

ma-MENCH-ih-SAW-rus
Mamenchin (a place in China)
reptile
Saurischia: Sauropoda
Late Jurassic
South-central China

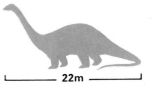

22m

Mamenchisaurus was a large sauropod related to APATOSAURUS and DIPLODOCUS. It was only known from some partial skeletons until a nearly complete specimen was found in 1972. This revealed something extraordinary. *Mamenchisaurus* had the longest neck of any animal that has ever lived. The neck was as long as the rest of the body. Out of a total length of 22 metres, 11 metres were neck! There were nineteen vertebrae in the neck – the highest number for any dinosaur – and it was strengthened by rods of bone. It may be that *Mamenchisaurus* stood in the middle of a pond and swept its head round the sides, eating up all the plants, with its neck floating on the water – like a giant vacuum cleaner.

Massospondylus

MASS-oh-SPOND-ih-lus
Massive vertebra
Saurischia: Prosauropoda
Late Triassic /early Jurassic
South Africa

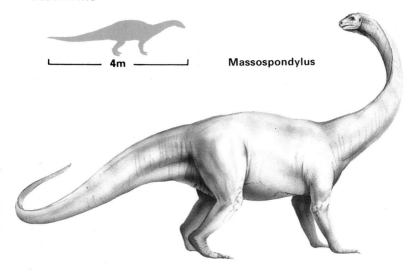

4m

Massospondylus

Massospondylus was a large animal, about 4 metres long, and one of the most widespread early dinosaurs. Its close relatives, which lived at the same time, were LUFENGOSAURUS in China and PLATEOSAURUS in Europe. *Massospondylus* was named in 1854 by Richard Owen from a few broken vertebrae that had been sent from South Africa to England. New fossils of *Massospondylus* were found later and there are now some partial skeletons which allow a reconstruction. *Massospondylus* had large strong hind legs. Its arms were also strong, and the hand could have been used for walking

or for grasping. The thumb was huge and it had a large curved claw. It could be placed against fingers two and three and might have been used for holding things. Fingers four and five were very small. A few odd bones from India have also been named as *Massospondylus*.

82

Megalosaurus

MEG-a-low-SAW-rus
Great reptile
Saurischia: Carnosauria
? Early Jurassic to early
Cretaceous
Europe, North Africa, Asia, South
America

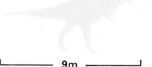

9m

Megalosaurus was the first dinosaur to be named – in 1824. The teeth of *Megalosaurus* had long roots that fixed them firmly into the jaw bone. The top of the tooth was curved backwards and flattened from side to side, and the back and front edges had jagged ridges, like the edge of a steak knife. The hand had three fingers, and the foot four toes, each with a strong claw, and *Megalosaurus* was obviously a fearsome predator. About 20 species of *Megalosaurus* have been described from rocks ranging in age over 100 million years. It is unlikely that one animal could have lived for so long, and many of the species have been based on very poor scraps that could belong to any meat-eating dinosaur.

Megalosaurus

83

Melanorosaurus

MEL-an-O-roe-SAW-rus
Black reptile
Saurischia: Prosauropoda
Late Triassic/early Jurassic
South Africa

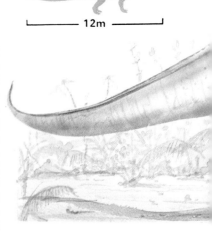

12m

Melanorosaurus was the largest early dinosaur. Its closest relative was EUSKELOSAURUS and some people think that the two animals are the same. *Melanorosaurus* probably walked on all fours, unlike its other relatives PLATEOSAURUS and LUFENGOSAURUS which may have stood upright at times. The original specimen was only a few limb bones and vertebrae – the reconstruction is based on these, and on related forms.

Monoclonius

MON-oh-KLONE-ee-us
One-horned
Ornithischia: Ceratopsia
Late Cretaceous
Alberta, Canada and western USA

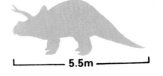

5.5m

Monoclonius was a medium-sized horned dinosaur about 5.5 metres long. It is known from several skeletons, and 11 species have been named. *Monoclonius* had a very large horn on its nose, but only slight bumps above its eyes (compare its head with TRICERATOPS). The frill was short and its back edge was covered with bony knobs. There were also two bony spikes which pointed forwards from the back of the frill.

Monoclonius

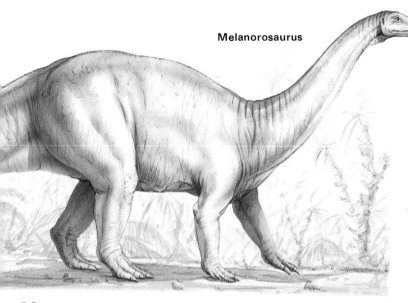

Melanorosaurus

Mussaurus

muss-AW-rus
Mouse reptile
Saurischia: ? Prosauropoda
Late Triassic
Argentina

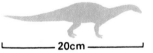

20cm

Mussaurus was named in 1979, based on five or six small skeletons. These were found together in a nest with the remains of two eggs. The largest skeleton was 20 centimetres long – about the size of a young kitten. The skeleton shows that *Mussaurus* was a prosauropod.

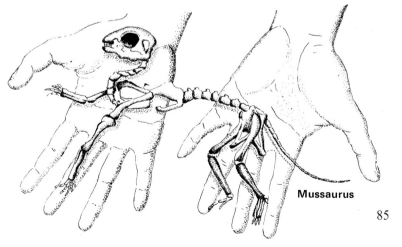

Mussaurus

85

Muttaburrasaurus

MUT-a-BUR-a-SAW-rus
Muttaburra (where found) reptile
Ornithischia: Ornithopoda
Late Cretaceous
Queensland, Australia

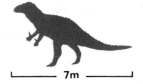

7m

Muttaburrasaurus is one of the very few dinosaurs known from Australia. It is a recent find and was named in 1981. *Muttaburrasaurus* was 7 metres long and it was related to IGUANODON or to CAMPTOSAURUS. It had a low, broad head, and it has been suggested that its teeth could have been used for chopping plants or meat. Earlier Australian dinosaurs show close similarities with African and American ones, but by the late Cretaceous, Australia may have had its own particular animals. Like most Late Cretaceous ornithopods, *Muttaburrasaurus* was larger than its Early Jurassic counterparts.

Nemegtosaurus

Nemegtosaurus

nem-EGT-oh-SAW-rus
Nemegt (where found) reptile
Saurischia: Sauropoda
Late Cretaceous
Mongolia

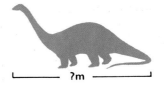

?m

Nemegtosaurus is known only from a skull that looks like that of DIPLODOCUS. The skull is long and slopes forward. If *Nemegtosaurus* is a diplodocid, it lived much later than its relatives which all come from rocks dated at 50 million years older. The headless skeleton of another sauropod, OPISTHOCOELICAUDIA, was found in the same deposit as the head of *Nemegtosaurus*, and it has been suggested that the two might go together as one animal. In any case, they would have been very similar.

Noasaurus

NOE-a-SAW-rus
Northwest Argentina reptile
Saurischia: ? Deinonychosauria
Late Cretaceous
Argentina

3m

Noasaurus was a medium-sized, active hunting dinosaur. It had a fierce hooked claw on its foot, just as in DEINONYCHUS and DROMAEOSAURUS, and it used this to attack other dinosaurs. *Noasaurus* was named in 1980, and it turned out to have a skull that is rather different from that of *Deinonychus*.

Nodosaurus

NODE-oh-SAW-rus
Node reptile
Ornithischia: Ankylosauria
Late Cretaceous
Kansas and Wyoming, USA

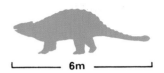

6m

Nodosaurus was a medium-sized armoured dinosaur related to PANOPLOSAURUS and SILVISAURUS. It had an armour of small bony knobs which were set in its skin all over the body. On the back and hip region were some oval-shaped plates which had small spines. These bony plates and spines were not attached to the bones of the skeleton: they sat in the animal's tough skin. This makes it difficult to know exactly how they were arranged. *Nodosaurus* was 5–6 metres long.

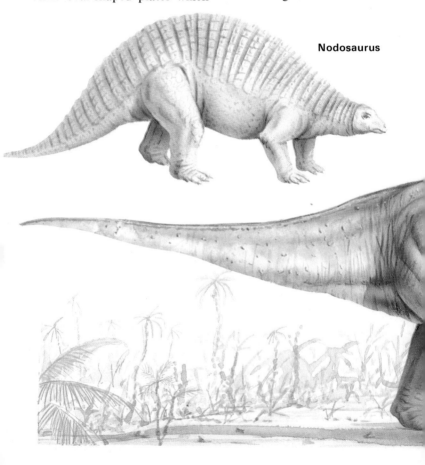

Nodosaurus

Opisthocoelicaudia

oh-PIS-thoe-SEEL-ih-KOW-dee-a
Tail bones hollow at the back
Saurischia: Sauropoda
Late Cretaceous
Mongolia

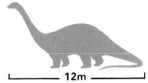

⊢——— 12m ———⊣

Opisthocoelicaudia was a moderate-sized sauropod, about 12 metres long. Only the skeleton is known, but this shows that it was related to CAMARASAURUS and EUHELOPUS. The head and neck of *Opisthocoelicaudia* were not found, and it has been suggested that the NEMEGTOSAURUS head might belong with it. The tail bones of *Opisthocoelicaudia* show that it might have been able to use its tail to grasp things, or to act as a prop.

ORNITHISCHIA

OR-nith-ISS-kee-a
Bird hips
Late Triassic to late Cretaceous
Worldwide

The Order Ornithischia includes a broad range of dinosaurs, all of which were plant-eaters. There were two-legged animals like IGUANODON and the duck-bills (ornithopods), the thick-headed dinosaurs (pachycephalosaurs), and the three groups of armoured dinosaurs (stegosaurs, ankylosaurs and ceratopsians).
Suborder Ornithopoda
Suborder Pachycephalosauria
Suborder Stegosauria
Suborder Ankylosauria
Suborder Ceratopsia

Opisthocoelicaudia

Ornitholestes

or-NITH-oh-LESS-teez
Bird robber
Saurischia: Coelurosauria
Late Jurassic
Wyoming, USA

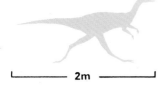

2m

Ornitholestes was a small lightly built meat-eater. An almost complete skeleton shows that it was 2 metres long. The legs and arms were slim and long. *Ornitholestes* had small teeth and rather weak hands. It was clearly a fast runner, and may have fed on small animals like lizards, frogs and early mammals, which lived at that time. *Ornitholestes* is very similar to COELURUS.

Ornitholestes

ORNITHOMIMOSAURIA

or-NITH-oh-MIME-oh-SAW-ree-a
Bird mimic reptiles
Saurischia
Late Jurassic to late Cretaceous
North America, Asia, Africa

The Infraorder Ornithomimosauria includes a group of advanced active running dinosaurs. They had small heads with no teeth, huge eyes and a long slim neck. The hind legs were long and thin, and the arms were delicate. The tail was long and thin. They must have looked very like featherless ostriches, and may have fed on animals and plants.

Family Ornithomimidae

? AVIMIMUS, ELAPHROSAURUS, GALLIMIMUS, ORNITHOMIMUS,
? OVIRAPTOR, STRUTHIOMIMUS

Ornithomimus

or-NITH-oh-MIME-us
Bird mimic
Saurischia: Ornithomimosauria
Late Cretaceous
Western Canada and USA

4m

Ornithomimus was a medium-sized ostrich dinosaur. More than half of its length of 3–4 metres was tail. Many skeletons and odd bones of *Ornithomimus* have been found, and ten species have been described. *Ornithomimus* had no teeth, but probably had a horny beak. It may have gathered food such as leaves, fruit, roots, insects, lizards and small mammals using its long strong fingers. It could chop these and swallow them in chunks, just as birds do.

Ornithomimus

ORNITHOPODA
OR-nith-oh-PODE-a
Bird feet
Ornithischia
Late Triassic to late Cretaceous
Worldwide

The Suborder Ornithopoda includes 60–70 different plant-eating dinosaurs. They stood on their hind legs, and most of them had no teeth right at the front of their jaws.

Family Fabrosauridae
    FABROSAURUS,
    SCUTELLOSAURUS
Family Heterodontosauridae
    GERANOSAURUS,
    HETERODONTOSAURUS,
    LYCORHINUS
Family Hypsilophodontidae
    DRYOSAURUS,
    HYPSILOPHODON,
    OTHNIELIA, PARKSOSAURUS,
    ?TROÖDON,
    ZEPHYROSAURUS
Family Iguanodontidae
    CAMPTOSAURUS,
    IGUANODON,
    MUTTABURRASAURUS,
    OURANOSAURUS
Family Hadrosauridae
    ANATOSAURUS,
    BRACHYLOPHOSAURUS,
    CLAOSAURUS, CORYTHO-
    SAURUS, EDMONTOSAURUS,
    HADROSAURUS, HYPA-
    CROSAURUS, LAMBEO-
    SAURUS, MAIASAURA, PARA-
    SAUROLOPHUS, PRO-
    SAUROLOPHUS, SAURO-
    LOPHUS, SECERNOSAURUS,
    SHANTUNGOSAURUS,
    TSINTAOSAURUS

Othnielia
OTH-nee-EL-ee-a
Named after Othniel C. Marsh, the dinosaur collector
Ornithischia: Ornithopoda
Late Jurassic
Western USA

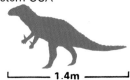

└─────── 1.4m ───────┘

Othnielia was a small dinosaur, only 1.4 metres long. It was very similar to HYPSILOPHODON, but there were small differences in the teeth. It was originally named as *Nanosaurus* by O. C. Marsh in 1877, and was renamed exactly one hundred years later.

Ouranosaurus
oo-RAN-oh-SAW-rus
Brave reptile
Ornithischia: Ornithopoda
Early Cretaceous
Niger, West Africa

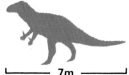

└─────── 7m ───────┘

Ouranosaurus is one of the most interesting dinosaurs from North Africa. It was related to IGUANODON, but had a tall sail down its back. The sail was supported by a fence of the spines of the backbone – one on each vertebra. The sail was made of skin, and blood vessels must have flowed through it. It may have been used by *Ouranosaurus* to keep its body temperature constant. If it was too hot, it could lose heat through the sail, and if it was too cold, it could take in heat from the sun. Another dinosaur with a sail was the meat-eater SPINOSAURUS.

Oviraptor

OVE-ih-RAP-tor
Egg thief
Saurischia: ? Ornithomimosauria
Late Cretaceous
Southern Mongolia

|————— 1.8m —————|

Oviraptor was an unusual small coelurosaur. The first skeleton was found in 1923 just above a nest of PROTOCERATOPS eggs, and it was thought that *Oviraptor* was an egg-eater for this reason. It had a short head and a powerful toothless beak. The jaws were curved so that it could crush very hard objects. *Oviraptor* had strong three-fingered hands with large claws which may have been useful in grasping. *Oviraptor* may have eaten eggs, but the powerful beak suggests it may have crushed bones.

Ouranosaurus

PACHYCEPHALOSAURIA

PAK-ee-KEF-al-oh-SAW-ree-a
Thick-headed reptiles
Ornithischia
Cretaceous
England, North America, Asia,
Madagascar

The Suborder Pachycephalosauria was only recently named for a group of two-legged plant-eating dinosaurs that had enormously thick skull roofs. The skull roof was up to 25 centimetres thick, and for that reason, this part of the animal is easily fossilized. Many of the bone-heads are only known from the skull roofs.

Family Pachycephalosauridae
   HOMALOCEPHALE,
   PACHYCEPHALOSAURUS,
   STEGOCERAS

Pachycephalosaurus

PAK-ee-KEF-al-oh-SAW-rus
Thick-headed reptile
Ornithischia: Pachycephalosauria
Late Cretaceous
Western North America

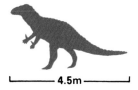

4.5m

Pachycephalosaurus was a very large bone-head. It was probably far bigger than its relatives – up to 4.5 metres long – although its skeleton is not known. The skull had a very thick top, just behind and above the eyes, and it was ornamented with knobs and spines. It seems that *Pachycephalosaurus* used its crash helmet head in fighting with other members of its own species. Today, male deer and goats batter each other head-on in fighting for mates.

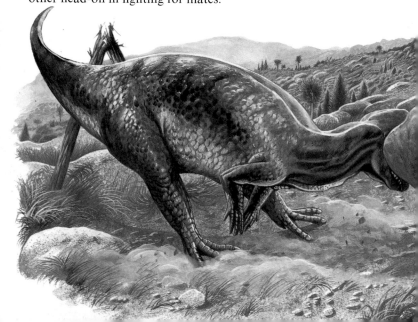

Pachyrhinosaurus

PAK-ee-RINE-oh-SAW-rus
Thick-nosed reptile
Ornithischia: Ceratopsia
Late Cretaceous
Alberta, Canada

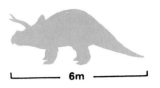

6m

Pachyrhinosaurus is one of the most unusual horned dinosaurs. It is known from four skulls and some other pieces. *Pachyrhinosaurus* had no horns, but only a thick mass of bone in the middle of its snout, between the eyes. There was a short neck frill at the back of the skull. *Pachyrhinosaurus* was a large animal: its skull alone measured up to 1.4 metres long, and its body may have been 6 metres long.

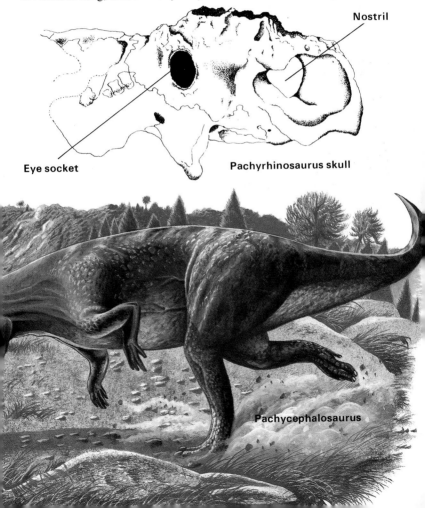

Nostril

Eye socket

Pachyrhinosaurus skull

Pachycephalosaurus

Panoplosaurus

pan-o-ploe-SAW-rus
Fully armoured reptile
Ornithischia: Ankylosauria
Late Cretaceous
Alberta, Canada and Texas, USA

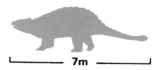

7m

Panoplosaurus was one of the last surviving ankylosaurs. It is known from a partial skull and skeleton. Its head was massive, and the top of the skull was arched and covered with large armour plates. *Panoplosaurus* had a narrow snout and small ridged teeth, and it may have fed by selecting plants at ground level.

Parasaurolophus

par-a-SAWR-oh-LOAF-us
Reptile with parallel-sided crest
Ornithischia: Ornithischia
Late Cretaceous
Alberta, Canada, Utah and New
Mexico, USA

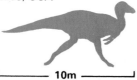

10m

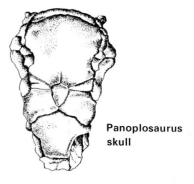

Panoplosaurus skull

Parasaurolophus was one of the most bizarre duck-billed dinosaurs. It had a long tubular crest that curved back from its snout for a distance of up to 1.8 metres. The nostrils were in their normal place at the front of the snout, and the breathing tubes ran right up the crest and back down again into the mouth. If you cut the crest open, you would find four tubes – two going up and two coming down. The crest may have been a signal to let other *Parasaurolophus* recognize a member of their own species. Also, if *Parasaurolophus* breathed out strongly, it could have made a honk or bellow inside the crest (SEE ALSO page 165).

Parksosaurus

PARKS-oh-SAW-rus
Parks' (Canadian palaeontologist)
reptile
Ornithischia: Ornithopoda
Late Cretaceous
Alberta, Canada

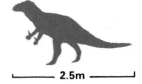

2.5m

Parksosaurus was one of the last surviving hypsilophodontids. Its earlier relatives include DRYOSAURUS, HYPSILOPHODON and ZEPHYRO-SAURUS. *Parksosaurus* is known from an incomplete skeleton. When this animal died, it was buried on its left side in the sand, and most of the right-hand side of the skeleton was broken up and lost. *Parksosaurus* had large eyes and a relatively short thigh bone. *Parksosaurus* was about 2.5 metres long.

Parasaurolophus

97

Pelorosaurus

pel-O-roe-SAW-rus
Monstrous reptile
Saurischia: Sauropoda
Late Jurassic and early
Cretaceous
Western Europe

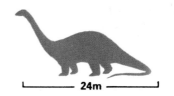
24m

Pelorosaurus was a large animal, related to BRACHIOSAURUS and SUPERSAURUS. This name was given in 1850 to a partial arm bone from Sussex, southern England. Since then, dozens of scraps of sauropods of about the same age were given the name *Pelorosaurus*: about twenty species in all were named. It is a common problem that the poorer the specimens of fossils are, the more names they are given. *Pelorosaurus* may have had an armour of little bone plates (1–3 centimetres across) sunk into its skin.

Pentaceratops

PEN-ta-SER-a-tops
Five-horned face
Ornithischia: Ceratopsia
Late Cretaceous
New Mexico, USA

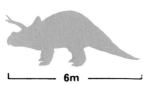
6m

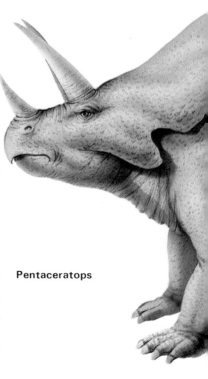

Pentaceratops had more horns than the other horned dinosaurs – five in all. It had one on its snout, one above each eye, and one on each cheek, at the bottom of the frill. This array of horns was used for defence against meat-eating dinosaurs. It is also likely that *Pentaceratops* used its horns for display. The neck frill was very long, and the back edge was knobbly. *Pentaceratops* was related to ANCHICERATOPS and TOROSAURUS, and it may have been 6 metres long.

Pentaceratops

Pinacosaurus

pin-AK-oh-SAW-rus
Plank reptile
Ornithischia:Ankylosauria
Late Cretaceous
Mongolia and northern China

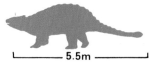

5.5m

Pinacosaurus was a large lightly built armoured dinosaur. It had a rounded beak and the top of its skull was covered with small bony plates. Its eye was set quite far back, and its teeth were very small. *Pinacosaurus* is remarkable for a pair of small openings in the skull near the nostrils. The purpose of these is not known. *Pinacosaurus* is related to ANKYLOSAURUS and DYOPLOSAURUS, and was 5.5 metres long.

Pinacosaurus skull

99

Plateosaurus

PLAT-ee-oh-SAW-rus
Flat reptile
Saurischia: Prosauropoda
Late Triassic
Germany, France, Switzerland

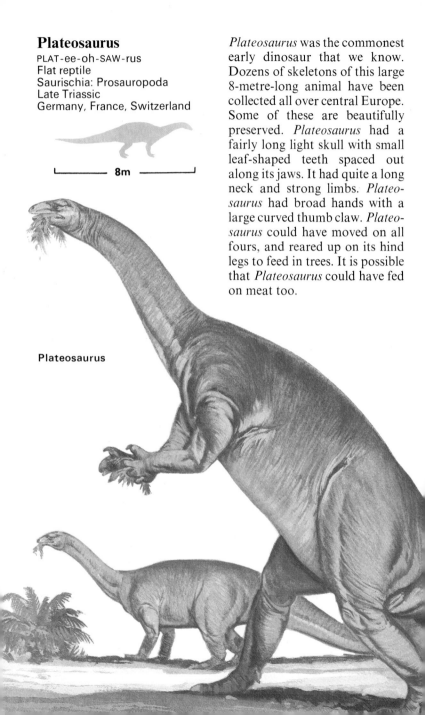

8m

Plateosaurus

Plateosaurus was the commonest early dinosaur that we know. Dozens of skeletons of this large 8-metre-long animal have been collected all over central Europe. Some of these are beautifully preserved. *Plateosaurus* had a fairly long light skull with small leaf-shaped teeth spaced out along its jaws. It had quite a long neck and strong limbs. *Plateosaurus* had broad hands with a large curved thumb claw. *Plateosaurus* could have moved on all fours, and reared up on its hind legs to feed in trees. It is possible that *Plateosaurus* could have fed on meat too.

Procompsognathus

PRO-comp-sow-NAY-thus
Before *Compsognathus*
Saurischia: Coelurosauria
Late Triassic
Southern Germany

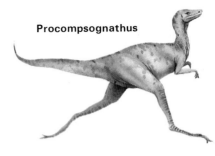
Procompsognathus

L———— 1m ————J

Procompsognathus was a very small early dinosaur. It was an agile running meat-eater that probably fed on small lizard-like animals and insects. The skull of *Procompsognathus* was only 8 centimetres long; it had large eyes and pointed curved teeth. *Procompsognathus* is related to COELOPHYSIS, SALTOPUS and SYNTARSUS.

Prosaurolophus

PRO-sawr-oh-LOAF-us
Before Saurolophus
Ornithischia: Ornithopoda
Late Cretaceous
Alberta, Canada

L———— 8m ————J

Prosaurolophus was a large duck-billed dinosaur, up to 8 metres long. The skull was low and had a small crest which ran up from the tip of the snout. There was a small knob at the top of this. *Prosaurolophus* is supposed to have been ancestral to SAUROLOPHUS which lived about five million years later.

PROSAUROPODA

PRO-sawr-oh-PODE-a
Before the sauropods
Saurischia
Late Triassic to early Jurassic
Worldwide

The Infraorder Prosauropoda includes a selection of early medium and large-sized dinosaurs. They are thought to include the ancestors of the giant sauropods, although this idea is still controversial.

Family Anchisauridae
ANCHISAURUS, ? ISCHISAURUS, ? STAURIKOSAURUS, THECODONTOSAURUS

Family Plateosauridae
AMMOSAURUS, LUFENGOSAURUS, MASSOSPONDYLUS, ? MUSSAURUS, PLATEOSAURUS

Family Melanorosauridae
EUSKELOSAURUS, MELANOROSAURUS, ? VULCANODON

101

Protoceratops

pro-toe-SER-a-tops
First horned-face
Ornithischia: Ceratopsia
Late Cretaceous
Mongolia

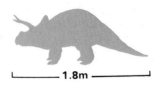

L——— 1.8m ———⌐

Protoceratops is the best known early horned dinosaur. Many skeletons were collected during an early American expedition to Mongolia in 1922. Some of these were found with complete nests of eggs, and this first showed us how dinosaurs cared for their young (SEE page 160). There were skeletons of baby *Protoceratops*, some still unhatched within the eggs. Adult *Protoceratops* was 1.8 metres long: the babies were 30 centimetres long. *Protoceratops* had a horny beak and a small neck frill. Its closest relatives were BAGACERATOPS, LEPTOCERATOPS, and MICROCERATOPS.

Protoceratops

Psittacosaurus

si-TAK-oh-SAW-rus
Parrot reptile
Ornithischia: Ceratopsia
Early Cretaceous
Mongolia and China

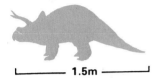

⊢——— **1.5m** ———⊣

Psittacosaurus is an interesting animal: it seems to be partly an ornithopod and partly a horned dinosaur. *Psittacosaurus* had long hind legs and shorter arms, so that it probably walked upright like IGUANODON. However, the skull was a little like that of an early ceratopsian (e.g. LEPTOCERATOPS). *Psittacosaurus* had a horny beak, a deep jaw, and a small frill at the back made from short spines pointing backwards. One species had a small horn on its nose. Some baby *Psittacosaurus* have been found recently and these were only 25 centimetres long. The adults were 1.5 metres long.

Psittacosaurus

Rhoetosaurus

REET-oh-SAW-rus
Rhoetos (A Greek mythical giant)
reptile
Saurischia: Sauropoda
Middle Jurassic
Australia

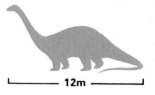
12m

Rhoetosaurus is a poorly known early sauropod from Australia. The skeleton was dug up in two parts: a tail in 1924, and the hip region in 1926. These bones were not enough to allow a reconstruction of *Rhoetosaurus*, but its length has been estimated as 12 metres. Its thigh bone was 1.5 metres long. *Rhoetosaurus* is one of the oldest sauropods and it is probably related to CETIOSAURUS.

Saltasaurus

SALT-a-SAW-rus
Salta (where found) reptile
Saurischia: Sauropoda
Late Cretaceous
Argentina

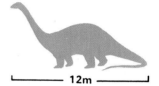
12m

Saltasaurus was a large armoured sauropod. Five incomplete skeletons of this animal were found in the late 1970s and these show that it was related to ANTARCTOSAURUS and TITANOSAURUS. The most interesting thing about *Saltasaurus* was that thousands of small and large bone plates were found with the skeletons. The small plates were only 5 millimetres or so across and they were packed closely in the skin to cover the whole body. The large plates were up to 10 centimetres across, and they had a ridge in the middle. These were scattered across the back amongst the smaller plates. *Saltasaurus* was 12 metres long.

A herd of Saltopus

Saltopus

SALT-oh-pus
Leaping foot
Saurischia: Coelurosauria
Late Triassic
Northern Scotland

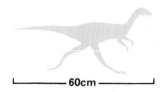

|————— 60cm —————|

Saltopus is one of the oldest dinosaurs known. It was named in 1910 from a small skeleton found in a sandstone quarry. *Saltopus* was an agile little animal, only 60 centimetres long, and it may have fed on small lizard-like animals and insects. *Saltopus* had long hind legs, and it was thought to be a jumping animal. However, it probably simply ran, like its relatives COELOPHYSIS and PROCOMPSOGNATHUS.

SAURISCHIA

sawr-ISS-kee-a
Reptile hips
Late Triassic to late Cretaceous
Worldwide

The Order Saurischia includes all the meat-eating dinosaurs, and the large heavy long-necked plant-eaters. It is divided into two suborders, the Theropoda (small and large meat-eaters), and the Sauropodomorpha (medium and large plant-eaters). It is likely that these two suborders of the Saurischia arose from rather different ancestors, because their distinguishing character, the 'lizard hip' was primitive. The main groups of saurischian dinosaurs are listed under 'Theropoda' and 'Sauropodomorpha' in this dictionary.

Saurolophus

SAW-oh-LOAF-us
Ridged reptile
Ornithischia: Ornithopoda
Late Cretaceous
North America and Asia

— 10m —

Saurolophus was an advanced crested, duck-billed dinosaur. It is known from several skeletons which show an animal about 9–10 metres long. *Saurolophus* had a large head with a pointed crest running backwards. The snout was broad, and the top of the head sloped backwards as a flat surface. Above the eyes, the skull bones continued backwards as a spike which stuck out behind the head. The North American and Asian species of *Saurolophus* were very similar except that the Asian one had a longer skull and a longer crest.

106

SAUROPODA

SAWR-oh-PODE-a
Reptile feet
Saurischia
Early Jurassic to late Cretaceous
Worldwide

The Infraorder Sauropoda includes all of the really big long-necked plant-eating dinosaurs. There were probably five main groups which can be told apart by features of the backbone (vertebrae), legs and head: the cetiosaurids (short head, front legs shorter than hind legs, solid vertebrae), the brachiosaurids (low snout, front legs longer than hind legs), the camarasaurids (short head, front legs shorter than hind legs, hollow vertebrae), the titanosaurids (steep long head, front legs shorter than hind legs, slightly hollowed vertebrae), and the diplodocids (long low head, front legs shorter than hind legs, hollow vertebrae).

Family Cetiosauridae
> ? BARAPASAURUS, CETIO-
> SAURUS, RHOETOSAURUS

Family Brachiosauridae
> BRACHIOSAURUS, PELORO-
> SAURUS, 'SUPERSAURUS'

Family Camarasauridae
> CAMARASAURUS,
> EUHELOPUS,
> OPISTHOCOELICAUDIA

Family Titanosauridae
> ALAMOSAURUS, ANTARCTO-
> SAURUS, HYPSELOSAURUS,
> SALTASAURUS, TITANO-
> SAURUS

Family Diplodocidae
> APATOSAURUS, BAROSAURUS,
> DICRAEOSAURUS, DIPLO-
> DOCUS, MAMENCHISAURUS,
> NEMEGTOSAURUS

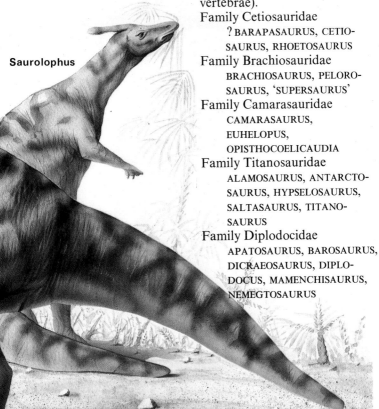

Saurolophus

SAUROPODOMORPHA

SAWR-oh-PODE-a-MORF-a
Reptile-foot forms
Saurischia
Late Triassic to late Cretaceous
Worldwide

The Suborder Sauropodomorpha is a division of the Order Saurischia, the 'lizard-hipped' dinosaurs. It includes two groups of medium and large plant-eating dinosaurs: the Infraorder Prosauropoda (early plant-eating, or possibly plant and meat-eating, animals with quite long necks), and the Infraorder Sauropoda (later large, four-legged plant-eaters with long necks).

Saurornithoides

sawr-OR-nith-OID-eez
Bird-like reptile
Saurischia: ? Deinonychosauria
Late Cretaceous
Mongolia

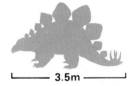

2m

Saurornithoides is a poorly known agile and intelligent small meat-eater. *Saurornithoides* had a long low head with small sharp teeth. It had a large eye and a very big brain for a reptile. The large brain allowed *Saurornithoides* to act and move quickly and to behave more intelligently than other dinosaurs.

Scelidosaurus

skel-IDE-oh-SAW-rus
Limb reptile
Ornithischia: ? Stegosauria
Early Jurassic
Southern England

3.5m

Scelidosaurus is a strange early armoured dinosaur. It was named from a collection of leg bones and a partial skull. It has now been shown that the leg bones come from a different animal – a megalosaur. Some new skeletons of *Scelidosaurus* have been found recently. *Scelidosaurus* had a small head with leaf-like ridged teeth. It had four strong legs and its body was armoured with bony knobs and spikes.

Scelidosaurus

Scutellosaurus

skoot-EL-oh-SAW-rus
Small-scaled reptile
Ornithischia: Ornithopoda
Early Jurassic
Arizona, USA

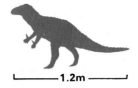

— 1.2m —

Scutellosaurus is an interesting early ornithopod that was named in 1981. *Scutellosaurus* had a short skull with ridged plant-eating teeth. Its hind legs were longer than the arms, but by a smaller amount than in most ornithopods. *Scutellosaurus* had a very long tail – about one-and-a-half times its total length of 1.2 metres. *Scutellosaurus* was armoured with hundreds of small bony knobs set in the skin of its back. This kind of armour has not been found in its relatives, like FABROSAURUS.

Secernosaurus

se-SER-no-SAW-rus
Separate reptile
Ornithischia: Ornithopoda
Late Cretaceous
Argentina

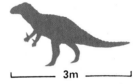

— 3m —

Secernosaurus is one of the few duck-billed dinosaurs known from South America. Most duck-bills lived in North America and Asia, and this South American duck-bill shows that there was a land connection which dinosaurs could cross. *Secernosaurus* probably had a flat head like EDMONTOSAURUS or SHANTUNGOSAURUS. The skeleton, named in 1979, shows that *Secernosaurus* was a small duck-bill, probably only 3 metres long.

Segisaurus

SEG-ih-SAW-rus
Segi Canyon (where found)
reptile
Saurischia: Coelurosauria
Early Jurassic
Arizona, USA

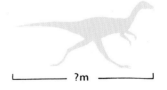

— ?m —

Segisaurus is a curious small early dinosaur. The incomplete skeleton is rather like PROCOMPSOGNATHUS in some features: the long slim hind leg and foot is very similar. However, the bones of *Segisaurus* are solid, whereas animals like *Procompsognathus* and COELOPHYSIS have hollow bones. *Segisaurus* was probably an active runner and meat-eater, but this is not certain.

SEGNOSAURIA

SEG-no-SAW-ree-a
Slow reptiles
Saurischia
Late Cretaceous
Asia

The Infraorder Segnosauria was named in 1980 for some strange new dinosaurs that had just been found in Mongolia. These were lightly built meat-eaters with curious skulls. The most unusual feature was the hip which was not at all like a typical saurischian 'lizard hip': the two bones at the bottom both ran backwards side-by-side, instead of one pointing forwards and the other backwards.

Family Segnosauridae
　　SEGNOSAURUS

Segnosaurus

SEG-no-SAW-rus
Slow reptile
Saurischia: Segnosauria
Late Cretaceous
Southern Mongolia

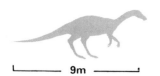

|———— 9m ————|

Segnosaurus is known from a skull and partial skeleton. The skull has sharp meat-cutting teeth at the back, but not teeth at the front of the jaw. This is very strange. Each foot had four toes, and the hip was quite unusual in shape. In *Segnosaurus*, the hip

looks rather like that of an ornithischian dinosaur, rather than a Saurischian. The primitive three-pointed 'lizard hip' has become a two-pointed 'bird hip'. However, in detail it is clear that

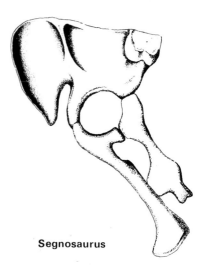

Segnosaurus

Segnosaurus is still a saurischian dinosaur. The scientists who named *Segnosaurus* in 1979 suggested that it might have been a swimmer and that it fed on fish.

Shantungosaurus

shan-TUNG-oh-SAW-rus
Shantung reptile
Ornithischia: Ornithopoda
Late Cretaceous
Shantung, China

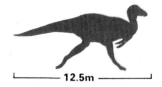

12.5m

Shantungosaurus was an advanced, flat-headed duck-billed dinosaur. It was the largest of this group, being over 12 metres long. It could have looked over the roof of a three-storey house. *Shantungosaurus* had a long, low skull, with a flat duck-shaped beak and no crest. A nearly complete skeleton of *Shantungosaurus* was discovered in the 1970s, and it is now on show in the Natural History Museum in Beijing (Peking), China. A grown man standing beside it just reaches the knee. (SEE ALSO page 137).

Shantungosaurus

111

Silvisaurus

SIL-vih-SAW-rus
Forest reptile
Ornithischia: Ankylosauria
Early Cretaceous
Kansas, USA

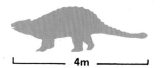

4m

Silvisaurus was a medium-sized armoured dinosaur. It was named in 1960 from a skull and partial skeleton which shows that it was 4 metres long. *Silvisaurus* had a heavy head, quite a long neck, and a bulky body. Its body was covered with an armour of flat honeycomb-shaped or round plates. There were some rounded spikes sticking out sideways on the tail and part of the body. *Silvisaurus* was related to NODOSAURUS and PANOPLOSAURUS.

Silvisaurus

Spinosaurus

SPINE-o-SAW-rus
Spiny reptile
Saurischia: Carnosauria
Late Cretaceous
Niger, Egypt

12m

Spinosaurus was a strange meat-eating dinosaur with a sail on its back. The sail was made from skin and it was held up by tall spines on the back of each vertebra of the backbone. Some of these spines were 2 metres high – taller than a human. *Spinosaurus* may have used its sail to control its body temperature: it could lose heat if it was too hot, or it could take in heat if it was too cold. *Spinosaurus* had typical meat-eating teeth, like steak-knives, but they were straight instead of curved. It was a giant animal, up to 12 metres long, and its closest relative may have been ACROCANTHOSAURUS.

Staurikosaurus

stor-IK-oh-SAW-rus
Cross reptile
Saurischia: ? Prosauropoda
Late Triassic
Brazil

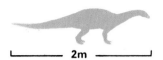

2m

Staurikosaurus was an early two-legged dinosaur. It was 2 metres long and had a light agile body. Its head was quite large and its teeth show that it probably ate meat. *Staurikosaurus* had long hind legs and shorter arms, all with five toes or fingers – which is a primitive feature. *Staurikosaurus* may have been related to early prosauropods like ANCHISAURUS and THECODONTOSAURUS, or to early coelurosaurs like COELOPHYSIS and PROCOMPSOGNATHUS.

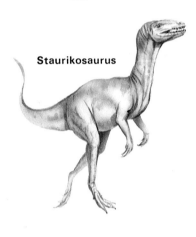

Staurikosaurus

Spinosaurus

Stegoceras

steg-O-ser-as
Horny roof
Ornithischia: Pachycephalosauria
Late Cretaceous
Western North America

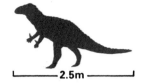

2.5m

Stegoceras was a medium-sized 2.5 metres long plant-eater with a very curious thick skull. It had a heavy skull covered with horny lumps and knobs. The top of the skull was very thick and it formed a high crest. This crest grew higher as *Stegoceras* grew older.

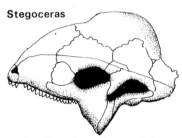

Stegoceras

STEGOSAURIA

STEG-oh-SAW-ree-a
Roofed reptiles
Ornithischia
? Early Jurassic to late Cretaceous
Worldwide

The Suborder Stegosauria includes a selection of medium and large-sized plant-eating dinosaurs. They all had an armour of spikes or plates, or both, along the middle of the back. Some also had spikes on their hips. There were two groups, the early scelidosaurids (which could be stegosaurs or ankylosaurs) and the later stegosaurids.
Family Scelidosauridae
    SCELIDOSAURUS
Family Stegosauridae
    DACENTRURUS, DRAVIDOSAURUS, KENTROSAURUS,
    LEXOVISAURUS, STEGOSAURUS

Stegosaurus

STEG-oh-SAW-rus
Roofed reptile
Ornithischia: Stegosauria
Colorado, Oklahoma, Utah and
Wyoming, USA

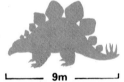

9m

Stegosaurus was named in 1877 from an incomplete skeleton from Colorado, USA. *Stegosaurus* had a tiny tubular skull with a brain the size of a walnut. Its teeth were small, blunt and leaf-like. *Stegosaurus* had small flat plates on its neck and bigger diamond-shaped plates on its back and the first part of its tail. These plates are usually shown in two rows, but it has been suggested recently that there was only a single row. At the end of the tail, *Stegosaurus* had four long spines. *Stegosaurus* had very short front legs, half the length of its hind legs. *Stegosaurus* was up to 9 metres long.

Stegosaurus

Stenonychosaurus

STEN-oh-NIKE-o-SAW-rus
Narrow-clawed reptile
Saurischia: Deinonychosauria
Late Cretaceous
Alberta, Canada

2m

Stenonychosaurus was probably the most intelligent dinosaur. It was a very lightly built animal, about 2 metres long, and with long slender legs and a long tail. It had fairly long arms with thin fingers. *Stenonychosaurus* was an agile and fast-moving meat-eater. The most interesting features of *Stenonychosaurus* are in the head. It had very large eyes and a large brain, equivalent to a bird of the same size. *Stenonychosaurus* was an active intelligent hunter with good senses and quick reflexes.

Struthiomimus

STROOTH-ee-oh-MIME-us
Ostrich mimic
Saurischia: Ornithomimosauria
Late Cretaceous
Alberta, Canada and New Jersey, USA

3.5m

Struthiomimus was shaped just like an ostrich, but without feathers. It was 3.5 metres long and had a very slender body. Its head was small and it had no teeth – only a horny beak. It had a long neck and a long tail which was used for balance. *Struthiomimus* was fast on its long hind legs and could have used its three-fingered hand to dig up food and to grasp things.

Stenonychosaurus

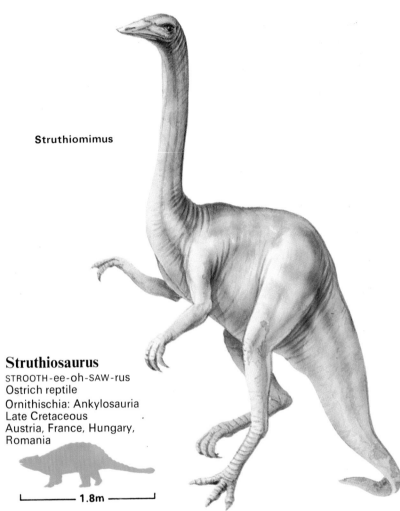

Struthiomimus

Struthiosaurus

STROOTH-ee-oh-SAW-rus
Ostrich reptile
Ornithischia: Ankylosauria
Late Cretaceous
Austria, France, Hungary,
Romania

⊢——— **1.8m** ———⊣

Struthiosaurus was the smallest known armoured dinosaur. At only 1.8 metres long, it was less than half the size of its relatives ACANTHOPHOLIS, HYLAEOSAURUS and NODOSAURUS. *Struthiosaurus* was also one of the last surviving ankylosaurs and it is unusual since it comes from Europe, rather than North America or Asia. *Struthiosaurus* had a small head and five different kinds of bony armour: plates with a big spine and small bones on the neck, a pair of very long spines on the shoulders, pairs of sloping plates on the hips and tail, and smaller spines and knobs on the sides of the body and tail.

117

Styracosaurus

STY-rak-oh-SAW-rus
Spiked reptile
Ornithischia: Ceratopsia
Late Cretaceous
Alberta, Canada and Montana,
USA

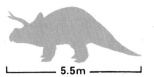

5.5m

Styracosaurus

Styracosaurus is a well-known horned dinosaur with a remarkable spiny frill. *Styracosaurus* was 5.5 metres long and it was probably related to MONOCLONIUS. The skull was long and it had six long spines that pointed back over the neck. It had a tall horn on its nose which pointed straight upwards. There were two much smaller horns above the eyes. This formidable array would have helped *Styracosaurus* to protect itself against predators and might also have warned off rivals of the same species.

Supersaurus

super-SAW-rus
Super reptile
Saurischia: Sauropoda
Late Jurassic
Colorado, USA

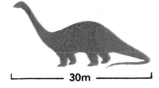

30m

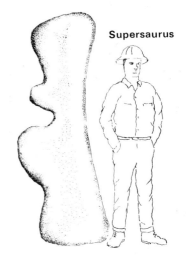

Supersaurus

'Supersaurus' has not been properly named yet, but it may have been the largest dinosaur known. The bones of 'Supersaurus' were discovered in 1971, and they clearly belonged to an animal like BRACHIOSAURUS. However, it was much bigger. One bone of the neck was over 1.5 metres long, and its shoulder blade was much longer than a man. It has been estimated that 'Supersaurus' was 30 metres long and 15 metres high. An even bigger animal, known as 'ULTRASAURUS' was found in 1979.

Syntarsus

sin-TAR-sus
Fused ankle
Saurischia: Coelurosauria
Late Triassic
Zimbabwe

3m

Syntarsus was an interesting small dinosaur. It was a lightly built 3-metre-long two-legged meat-eater. Syntarsus was rather like COELOPHYSIS except that some of its ankle bones were fused or joined together. Some scientists have reconstructed Syntarsus with a plume on the back of its head and a covering of feathers. This was because they wanted to prove that dinosaurs were warm-blooded like birds. There is no evidence for feathers in Syntarsus.

Syntarsus

Tarbosaurus

TAR-bo-SAW-rus
Reptile from Bataar
Saurischia: Carnosauria
Late Cretaceous
Mongolia

L_____ 14m _____J

Tarbosaurus was a large meat-eater, an Asian relative of TYRANNOSAURUS. It was about the same size as *Tyrannosaurus*, but less heavily built. *Tarbosaurus* had a longer skull and twenty-seven large curved knife-like teeth along its upper jaw. It had very short arms with only two fingers on each hand. *Tarbosaurus* was 10–14 metres long, and it could have fed on the duck-billed dinosaurs and armoured dinosaurs that lived with it in Mongolia.

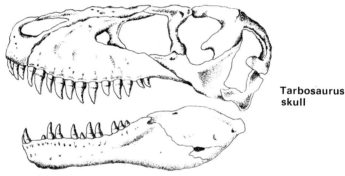

Tarbosaurus
skull

Thecodontosaurus

THEEK-oh-DON-to-SAW-rus
Socket-toothed reptile
Saurischia: Prosauropoda
Late Triassic /early Jurassic
England and South Africa

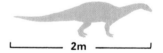

L_____ 2m _____J

Thecodontosaurus was an early medium-sized dinosaur. It was named in 1843 from a piece of jaw from Bristol, south-west England. *Thecodontosaurus* was 2 metres long and could have walked on all fours or upright. Its small light skull had many sharp leaf-like teeth that could have been used to eat plants or meat. *Thecodontosaurus*

had a long neck and strong arms with a big curved thumb claw. It was probably related to ANCHISAURUS.

Therizinosaurus

THER-ih-zin-oh-SAW-rus
Scythe reptile
Saurischia: ? Deinonychosauria
Late Cretaceous
Southern Mongolia

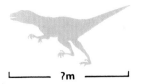

?m

Therizinosaurus was named recently for a huge arm with fierce claws found in Mongolia. The arm was about 2.5 metres long in all, and a single scythe-like claw was 70 centimetres round its outer curve. That makes the claw alone the size of a hand-held scythe used for cutting long grass, but the *Therizinosaurus* claw was much heavier. This dinosaur may be related to DEINOCHEIRUS.

THEROPODA

THER-oh-PODE-a
Beast feet
Saurischia
Early Jurassic to late Cretaceous
Worldwide

The Suborder Theropoda includes all of the small, medium and large-sized meat-eating dinosaurs. There were five main groups: the coelurosaurs (small and medium-sized, lightly built), the ornitho-mimosaurs (very slender, ostrich-like), the deinonychosaurs (lightly built, large fierce claws), the segnosaurs (with an unusual hip), and the carnosaurs (all the heavy medium and large forms).

Infraorder Coelurosauria
Infraorder Ornithomimosauria
Infraorder Deinonychosauria
Infraorder Segnosauria
Infraorder Carnosauria

Thecodontosaurus

121

Titanosaurus

tie-TAN-oh-SAW-rus
Titanic reptile
Saurischia: Sauropoda
Late Cretaceous
Europe, India, Indochina and
South America

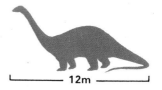

Titanosaurus was a medium-sized sauropod that was very widespread. Ten or more species of _Titanosaurus_ have been named from countries as far apart as India, Hungary and Argentina. The fact that this one dinosaur has been found in so many parts of the world shows that it was able to migrate freely. _Titanosaurus_ was about 12 metres long and rather heavily built. It had a long tail, a shorter neck and a broad back probably covered with armour, as in SALTASAURUS.

Torosaurus

TOR-oh-SAW-rus
Bull reptile
Ornithischia: Ceratopsia
Late Cretaceous
Western USA

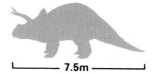

Torosaurus had the longest frill of all the horned dinosaurs. _Torosaurus_ had a horny beak, a small horn on its nose, and two large ones pointing forwards above its eyes. The frill at the back of the skull was longer than the skull itself. One specimen of _Torosaurus_ is a skull that is 2.6 metres long: this is the biggest head of any known land animal. The head alone was the size of a small car. _Torosaurus_ was about 7.5 metres long overall.

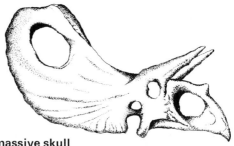

▶ **Torosaurus's massive skull** was up to 2.6 metres long from the tip of the skull to the back of the frill. That means it was larger than the skull of any other known land animal.

122

Triceratops

try-SER-a-tops
Three-horned face
Ornithischia: Ceratopsia
Late Cretaceous
Western Canada and USA

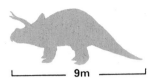

9m

Triceratops is the best known horned dinosaur. It was named in 1889 by O. C. Marsh (SEE page 133) on the basis of the skull. Two years earlier, Marsh had described a couple of *Triceratops* horns as coming from a fossil bison. Since then, nearly 20 species of *Triceratops* have been named, some on very poor material. *Triceratops* had three horns: one on its nose and two long ones above its eyes. Its neck frill was fairly short, and the back edge was surrounded by a zig-zag of knobs of bone. *Triceratops* was heavily built, with strong legs. Each finger or toe had a small hoof on the end. *Triceratops* was very large, measuring up to 9 metres long (SEE ALSO page 164).

Triceratops

Troödon

TROE-o-don
Wounding tooth
Ornithischia: Ornithopoda
Late Cretaceous
Alberta, Canada and Montana,
USA

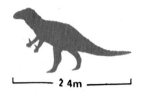

2 4m

Troödon is a poorly known and very unusual animal. A pointed saw-edged tooth was named *Troödon* in 1856, and in the 1940s more fossils seemed to show that it was the same as the bone-head STEGOCERAS. Recent discoveries in 1979 and 1980 show that *Troödon* may have been related to HYPSILOPHODON and PARKSOSAURUS. However, its teeth were sharp and like those of a meat-eater. If Troödon did eat meat, it would be the only ornithischian dinosaur to have done so.

Tsintaosaurus

SIN-tow-SAW-rus
Reptile from Tsintao
Ornithischia: Ornithopoda
Late Cretaceous
China

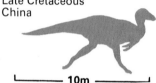

10m

Tsintaosaurus was a very strange duck-billed dinosaur. It had a tall horn on the top of its head, just between the eyes. The horn pointed forwards and it was hollow. The breathing tubes ran up the horn. *Tsintaosaurus* was large – about 10 metres long. It may be related to SAUROLOPHUS or to PARASAUROLOPHUS (SEE ALSO page 165).

Tsintaosaurus

124

Tyrannosaurus

tie-RAN-oh-SAW-rus
Tyrant reptile
Saurischia: Carnosauria
Late Cretaceous
Alberta, Canada and Montana,
USA

L———— **15m** ————⅃

Tyrannosaurus may be the best known dinosaur. It was certainly one of the biggest meat-eaters, and probably the most frightening that has ever lived. It was up to 15 metres long and 6 metres high: a man would hardly have reached its knee. *Tyrannosaurus* had a massive head which was 1.5 metres long. The powerful jaws were lined with large sharp teeth. Single teeth were up to 18 centimetres long: the size of a butcher's heavy chopping knife. *Tyrannosaurus* could probably have swallowed human beings whole if it was around today.

Tyrannosaurus

Ultrasaurus

ULL-tra-SAW-rus
Ultra reptile
Saurischia: Sauropoda
Late Jurassic
Colorado, USA

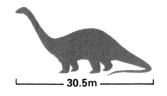

|— 30.5m —|

'Ultrasaurus' was discovered in 1979. It has not yet been given a scientific name. *'Ultrasaurus'* was probably even bigger than 'SUPERSAURUS', measuring up to 30.5 metres long.

Velociraptor

vel-O-si-RAP-tor
Fast thief
Saurischia: Deinonychosauria
Late Cretaceous
Mongolia

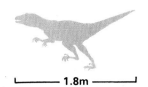

|— 1.8m —|

Velociraptor was a medium-sized lightly built meat-eater. *Velociraptor* had a long low skull, with a very flat snout. It had long arms and its legs were slender. One toe of each foot was large and scythe-like, as in DEINONYCHUS and DROMAEOSAURUS. In 1971 a specimen of *Velociraptor* was found that had died while attacking a PROTOCERATOPS. *Velociraptor* had a firm hold of the head-shield of *Protoceratops* and was kicking at the belly of *Protoceratops* with its

huge foot-claw. *Protoceratops* had pierced the chest region of *Velociraptor* with its armoured head. They must have killed each other at exactly the same time.

Vulcanodon
vul-KAN-oh-don
Volcano tooth
Saurischia: ? Prosauropoda
Late Triassic /early Jurassic
Zimbabwe

|—— 6.5m ——|

Vulcanodon is a strange animal that was named in 1972. Its teeth were like those of a prosauropod – small with serrated edges, while its limbs were like those of a sauropod. It could be related to MELANOROSAURUS or to CAMARASAURUS. *Vulcanodon* was about 6.5 metres long.

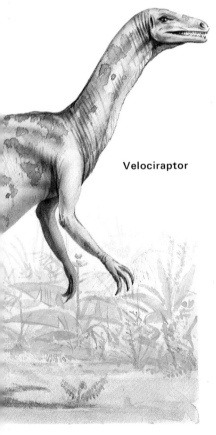

Velociraptor

Zephyrosaurus
zef-EYE-roe-SAW-rus
West-wind reptile
Ornithischia: Ornithopoda
Early Cretaceous
Montana, USA

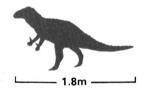

|—— 1.8m ——|

Zephyrosaurus was rather like HYPSILOPHODON, and is one of the few dinosaurs whose name begins with Z. It was named in 1980 from a skull and a vew vertebrae. *Zephyrosaurus* had small ridged teeth which were adapted for efficient chopping of plant food. *Zephyrosaurus* was a two-legged animal, about 1.8 metres long.

127

Collecting Dinosaurs

Dinosaur bones have been found all over the world and there are thousands in our museums today. Most of these bones have been collected only in the last 150 years. Before then nobody knew that dinosaurs had ever existed. So how were they discovered and who were the first people to study them?

Pioneers of the Past

Before 1820: Robert Plot

In the Middle Ages and even in Roman times there were people who collected shell and fish fossils. They must also have come across the huge bones of dinosaurs. Yet, surprisingly, the earliest description and drawing of a dinosaur bone was published as late as 1677. Robert Plot, an Oxford University professor, wrote a book called *The Natural History of Oxfordshire*, in which there was a drawing of a huge bone which had been found near Oxford. Although Plot's specimen has been lost, his drawing is good enough to show that it was the end of the thigh bone of MEGALOSAURUS.

Plot could only guess what the bone was and what he wrote is fairly typical of what people thought about fossils 300 years ago. Scientists

▶ **Dr Robert Plot,** who described the first dinosaur. He published the drawing below of the end of a *Megalosaurus* thigh bone in 1677. He thought it came from a giant man.

then had very different ideas about fossils and the history of life. At this time anything that was dug out of the ground was called a fossil. This included oddly shaped stones and pebbles, and even potatoes. In addition it was generally believed that the Earth was not particularly old. James Ussher, Archbishop of Armagh, went to great pains to discover the age of the Earth. From certain dates in the Bible, he calculated that the Earth was created at 8 o'clock in the evening on Saturday 3rd October, 4004 years before Christ. Few people at that time believed in extinction – the idea that species of animals and plants completely died out and nothing was known about prehistoric life.

So, it is not surprising that Plot did not even consider the possibility that his fossil might belong to an extinct animal. The idea never occurred to him. He first thought that the specimen might be an artificial stone, but then he realized that it was a real bone because of its shape and because he could see the internal structure of it. Could it, he wondered, be part of an elephant 'brought hither during the government of the Romans in Britain?' Plot rejected this idea after

▼ **Mrs Mary Mantell** found one of the first dinosaurs. She picked up a tooth of *Iguanodon* in southern England in 1822. Mrs Mantell was an artist, and she drew pictures of rocks and fossils for her husband's books about geology.

▼ **Dr Gideon Mantell** wrote about some of the first known dinosaurs. He named the tooth found by his wife, and some other bones, as *Iguanodon*. He collected bones and teeth in many parts of the south of England.

comparing his specimen with a living elephant that happened to be in Oxford at the time in a travelling menagerie. In the end he had to suggest – doubtfully – that it was the bone of a giant man or woman.

1820–1835: William Buckland and Gideon Mantell

In about 1818 a small collection of bones was obtained by William Buckland, the Professor of Geology at Oxford. These had been found at Stonesfield, a small quarrying village near Oxford. There was a jaw bone with long knife-like teeth, some limb bones, ribs and vertebrae. In 1824, Buckland published a description of these bones, and named them MEGALOSAURUS (giant reptile). This was the first dinosaur name to be published.

By 1820, ideas about fossils, the age of the Earth and extinction had advanced since the days of Robert Plot. Fossils were known to be the remains of ancient plants and animals. This became obvious as more and more fossils were discovered, and it was seen that they had all the details of the shells and bones of living animals. Geologists had come to realize that the Earth might be older than previously thought. Geologists had seen this when they made maps and calculated the great thicknesses of sedimentary rocks that had been deposited. They also knew something about extinction: huge bones of extinct mammoths were found from time to time. One theory was that these mammoths had all perished in the Great Flood of the Bible. It was possible to argue that there were still giant mammoths living somewhere on the Earth, but that we had not yet discovered them. Buckland knew that MEGALOSAURUS was an extinct reptile, and he called it the 'great fossil lizard of Stonesfield'. The famous bones that Buckland described in 1824 may still be seen in Oxford University Museum.

The second dinosaur to be named came from near Lewes in Sussex, south-east England and was discovered by Mary Ann Mantell. Mrs Mantell was out walking when she spotted an enormous fossil tooth in a pile of rubble beside the road. She took the tooth and showed it to her husband, Gideon Mantell, who was a doctor and also a keen fossil collector and geologist. He was excited by this find. He asked many experts what it might be and was told that it came from a big fish or from a rhinoceros. Mantell found more teeth and bones from this animal and finally saw that the teeth were very like those of the iguana, a large tropical American lizard, only much bigger. Mantell described some of these fossils in 1822 and gave a picture of the first teeth. However, he waited until he had more bones before naming it *Iguanodon* in 1825. In 1833 Mantell described the third dinosaur, the ankylosaur, HYLAEOSAURUS.

1835–1870: Richard Owen

It was Richard Owen who realized that MEGALOSAURUS, IGUANODON and HYLAEOSAURUS were not simply giant lizards as Buckland and Mantell had assumed. His studies led him to conclude that they belonged to a completely extinct group and in 1841 he invented the name 'dinosaur' for them. He argued that they were huge advanced animals quite different from all living reptiles.

When the Great Exhibition was held in London in 1851, Owen was asked to advise a painter and sculptor, Benjamin Waterhouse Hawkins, about the design of some life-sized models of MEGALOSAURUS, IGUANODON and HYLAEOSAURUS to be built out of bricks and tiles. The dinosaurs were modelled on all fours in the shape of a rhinoceros, and can still be seen.

▲ **Sir Richard Owen** invented the name 'dinosaur' in 1841. He wrote about many dinosaurs from England.

▼ **In 1851** some life-size models of the English dinosaurs were built for the Great Exhibition in London. This is how Owen thought *Iguanodon* looked. A special dinner was held inside the model.

DINNER IN THE IGUANODON MODEL, AT THE CRYSTAL PALACE, SYDENHAM.

In 1859 Charles Darwin published his famous book *On the Origin of Species by Means of Natural Selection*. In this, Darwin showed that the Earth was very ancient and that plants and animals had evolved over millions of years. He convinced most people that *evolution* had occurred by *natural selection* or 'survival of the fittest'. Darwin's ideas have had an enormous effect on the way we look at the history of life.

1830–1860: Edward Hitchcock and Joseph Leidy

In the early part of the 19th century some remarkable large three-toed footprints were found in the red sandstones of New England in the eastern United States. A local geologist, Edward Hitchcock wrote a book about them in 1858. He thought that the tracks belonged to giant birds, but we now know that these tracks were made by dinosaurs like AMMOSAURUS, ANCHISAURUS and MEGALOSAURUS.

The first dinosaur skeletons from North America were described in the 1850s. A professor of Anatomy called Joseph Leidy was the first American to reconstruct a dinosaur skeleton from bones found in New Jersey. He found that it was a new kind of dinosaur which he named HADROSAURUS in 1858. There was enough of the skeleton to show him that this dinosaur stood upright like a kangaroo, instead of on all fours, as Richard Owen had thought. The hind limbs of the skeleton were much longer than the forelimbs.

Leidy deduced from this that *Hadrosaurus* must have stood upright. So ths was the first proper reconstruction of a dinosaur. Leidy also identified several fossil teeth found in Montana by the geologist Ferdinand Hayden.

◀ **Three-toed footprints** like these were some of the first dinosaur remains found in North America. They were thought at first to have been made by giant birds that stood 5 metres tall.

1860–1900: Edward Cope and Othniel Marsh

The biggest collections of North American dinosaurs were made in the last decades of the 19th century by teams of professional bone collectors. These collectors were paid by two scientists who were deadly rivals, Edward Cope and Othniel Marsh.

The Cope and Marsh collectors discovered major new dinosaur beds in Montana, Colorado and Wyoming in the American mid-West. They sent loads of giant bones in giant crates. The two teams worked secretly and avoided each other. Cope and Marsh eagerly awaited the arrival of each crate of bones, and they rushed to be first to describe the new dinosaurs. This rivalry – the famous 'bone wars' – led to many scientific arguments between the two men, and often both of them gave different names to the same animal. Between them, Cope and Marsh described many important dinosaurs, such as ALLOSAURUS, APATOSAURUS (*Brontosaurus*), CAMARASAURUS, CAMPTOSAURUS, COELOPHYSIS, DIPLODOCUS, STEGOSAURUS, and TRICERATOPS.

Edward Cope

Othniel Marsh

1876–1900: Belgium

One of the most famous dinosaur discoveries was made in Belgium in 1878. Workmen found many large bones in a coal mine at Bernissart, 322 metres underground. In three years over thirty nearly complete skeletons were dug up and they were identified as IGUANODON. It seemed that a herd of IGUANODON had become trapped in marshy ground where they were all fossilized.

1900–1920: North America and East Africa

Cope and Marsh died before 1900, but many more collectors were now operating in North America. A millionaire named Andrew Carnegie was determined to have a skeleton of one of the biggest dinosaurs for his museum in Pittsburg, Pennsylvania. Between 1895 and 1905 he spent 25 million dollars on large fossil collecting trips. A complete skeleton of DIPLODOCUS was found for him in 1899 and

▲ **Carnegie's Diplodocus:** one of the best-known dinosaur skeletons. This skeleton was dug up about 1900, for the millionaire Andrew Carnegie. He had several casts of the skeleton made, and they can be seen in museums around the world.

Carnegie had life-size casts of it sent to the leading museums of the world.

One of the most important dinosaur finds of this period was made in 1909 by Earl Douglass, one of Carnegie's collectors. He found a complete *Apatosaurus* skeleton beside the Green River in Colorado and this was followed by the discovery of many more dinosaurs in the same area. In 1915 it was named Dinosaur National Monument. The bone bed has been cleared up and it has been made into a 'living museum' where visitors can see dinosaurs being excavated before their eyes. (SEE page 9).

The next 'dinosaur rush' in North America occurred along the Red Deer River in Alberta, Canada. Barnum Brown and Charles Sternberg led two teams and collected hundreds of specimens of typical late Cretaceous hadrosaurs, ceratopsians and carnosaurs such as ALBERTOSAURUS, ANATOSAURUS, CERATOSAURUS, CORYTHOSAURUS, DASPLETOSAURUS, EDMONTOSAURUS, MONOCLONIUS, PARA-SAUROLOPHUS, STYRACOSAURUS and TRICERATOPS.

The biggest dinosaur dig began in 1907 in Tanzania, then German East Africa. A German geologist was shown a huge dinosaur bone

▼ **A famous dinosaur dig in Africa.** Werner Janensch and a local workman look at a dinosaur bone at Tendaguru in Tanzania. From 1909 to 1912, 500 men worked to dig up 250 tonnes of fossils which were shipped back to Berlin, in Germany.

bed at Tendaguru, a remote area that was four days march from the nearest seaport. The Berlin museum raised a large sum of money and equipped an expedition. They employed 500 local labourers to dig up the bones. The leader of the expedition, Werner Janensch, worked there for four years and sent 250 tonnes of bones back to Berlin. These included complete skeletons of late Jurassic dinosaurs such as BRACHIOSAURUS, DICRAEOSAURUS, ELAPHROSAURUS and KENTRO-SAURUS. They had no transport and so the porters carried everything on their heads and backs. They carried food and supplies in and carried the bones out.

1920–1960: Germany, Mongolia

Some very early dinosaurs such as PLATEOSAURUS had been found in the late Triassic of Germany in the 19th century. In 1921 Friedrich von Huene directed an excavation at Trossingen which lies south of Tübingen and found thousands of bones of *Plateosaurus*. Many of the bones were well preserved, and it provided a complete picture of an important early dinosaur.

In 1922 an American expedition set off for Mongolia in Central Asia to find the ancestors of human beings. They did not find these but they did find some very important dinosaurs. They collected skeletons of PROTOCERATOPS, and also complete nests of its eggs. They found various hadrosaurs and other ceratopsians, as well as some important two-legged carnivores like OVIRAPTOR, SAURORNITHOIDES and VELOCIRAPTOR. In the late 1940s the Russians also sent expeditions to Mongolia and they brought back many crates of bones including specimens of SAUROLOPHUS and TARBOSAURUS.

1960 to the Present Day

In the last 25 years hundreds of dinosaur collecting expeditions have gone out. Large numbers of bones have been sent back to museums all over the world, and dozens of new forms have been described.

However, little new material has been found in Europe. In 1983 a carnivorous dinosaur with a huge claw about 30 centimetres long was dug up in Surrey in south-east England. This was named *Baryonyx* in 1986, meaning 'heavy claw'. Several important finds have been made in the United States and Canada, and recently named dinosaurs include DEINONYCHUS, MAIASAURA, OTHNIELIA, SCUTELLOSAURUS, 'SUPERSAURUS', and ZEPHYROSAURUS.

Some of the most exciting recent finds have been made in Asia. The late Cretaceous dinosaur beds of Mongolia have been excavated again and again by teams from Poland, Russia, and from Mongolia itself, bringing to light previously unknown dinosaurs such as

AVIMIMUS, DEINONYCHUS, HOMALOCEPHALE, SEGNOSAURUS, and THERIZINOSAURUS. The Chinese have also started excavating their dinosaur beds. They have found many new dinosaurs including MAMENCHISAURUS and TSINTAOSAURUS. Recent discoveries in India include BARAPASAURUS and DRAVIDOSAURUS.

There have recently been some very important excavations in South America where skeletons of MUSSAURUS, NOASAURUS, SALTASAURUS and SECERNOSAURUS have been unearthed. The dinosaur deposits of Australia are just being explored now, and they have yielded MUTTABURRASAURUS. Finally, French expeditions to North Africa have produced many new finds, including OURANO-SAURUS.

More dinosaurs are being found now at more sites in the world than ever before. The study of dinosaurs is hardly a dead subject! How then do scientists set about digging up a dinosaur and how do they study it?

▼ **A recent find from China.** The giant duck-billed dinosaur *Shantungosaurus* in the Beijing (Peking) Natural History Museum. A reconstruction is shown behind.

How to Collect a Dinosaur

There are two problems about digging up a dinosaur: they are usually found in places that are hundreds of miles from anywhere, and they are usually very big. In many ways we still use the same methods that Cope and Marsh's collectors used. The main difference is that they used horses to drag the enormous bones out, and we usually use motor vehicles now.

If a dinosaur collector sees a bone sticking out of the rock he tries to work out which bone it is. Then he can try to guess what other parts of the skeleton are still in the rock. First of all, the rock on top of the skeleton is taken off by machine or by hand. The last 15–20 centimetres or so are then taken off much more carefully. The bone collector uses small chisels, needles, and brushes, because he does not

◀ **Clearing the site.** When some bones have been found, many tons of rock may have to be taken off the skeleton. Drills, wedges and explosives may be used. The rock is cleared to just above the bones in this way.

◀ **The bones are exposed.** More careful methods are used to clean up the bones themselves. Small drills, chisels and needles are used. The whole skeleton is exposed and photographed to make a record of how it was found.

want to damage the bone. He tries to uncover the whole skeleton so that he can draw a detailed map of every bone as it lies in the rock. This is important for working out how the skeleton was buried, and for rebuilding the skeleton later.

Then the bone collector digs deep trenches round every bone, or group of bones. He covers each bone with cloth and plaster to protect it. When the plaster is dry, he digs under each bone and turns it over. He then clears out the rock under the bone and plasters over that. Each bone is wrapped up completely in plaster and they can now be carried back to the museum by truck or by train without any fear of damage. The bones of one ordinary dinosaur – say ANATOSAURUS – might weigh 10 or 20 tonnes when they are all wrapped in plaster. A DIPLODOCUS skeleton in plaster might weigh over 100 tonnes. It is difficult and expensive to dig up dinosaurs and take them to a museum.

◄ **Plastering the bones.** Each bone, or group of bones, is wrapped in bandages made from sack-cloth, and plaster. This protects the ancient bones, which may be fragile, and it makes them easier to handle.

◄ **Taking the dinosaur home.** The plastered blocks are loaded up and driven back to the museum, often a long way from the dinosaur site. Some of the plastered blocks are very heavy, and it takes a lot of work to move them.

Back at the museum. The plaster jackets are cut off the bones. Each bone is cleaned up with small drills and needles (top left). Extra casts may be made of the bones (bottom left). If the skeleton is good enough, it will be put on display. A metal frame has to be built to hold it up (top; right), and the bones and teeth have to be protected with special glues (right).

In the museum, the plaster is cut off the bones. They are cleaned up using needles, brushes and even acid. The bone is then hardened and strengthened with special glue.

Then a palaeontologist (fossil expert) sorts out the bones and tries to reconstruct or rebuild the skeleton. He uses the plan of the skeleton as it was found, and he compares it with other skeletons he has seen. At last the bones can be put in their proper places and they may be mounted for display. This means that a strong metal frame has to be built to hold all the bones up. The frame has to be very strong and it is very difficult to make. Look for the metal frames next time you are in a dinosaur museum.

The palaeontologist is interested in what the dinosaur was like when it was alive. He can see from the bones where the muscles and other soft parts went. He can work out how the animal fed from its

teeth and jaws and how it ran by looking at its legs. He will compare the skeleton with others to see if he has a new kind of dinosaur which would have to be named. Then he writes a description of the skeleton and includes drawings or photographs of all of the bones. He also gives a *reconstruction* of the whole animal if he can, and explains how it lived. Then other scientists can find out about the skeleton and it may be put into a dinosaur book like this one so that everyone can read about it.

Facts and Theories

How did the dinosaurs arise and why did they die out? Were they warm-blooded or not? How did they feed, move and behave? What were baby dinosaurs like? What was the reason for all the variety of frills, horns, spines, teeth and claws in the different groups? The answers to these questions form some of the most exciting areas of recent research on dinosaurs, and many of them are still open to debate. Even today scientists are unsure about some aspects of dinosaur life and many riddles remain unsolved. A single fossil find can sometimes provide us with exciting new evidence and provoke a new theory.

The Rise of the Dinosaurs

Dinosaur Origins

The oldest known dinosaurs were small coelurosaurs like SALTOPUS and STAURIKOSAURUS. These are found in Upper Triassic rocks from Scotland and South America dated at 225 million years old.

Dinosaurs were rather rare in northern Scotland at that time. Of every 150 reptiles, only one would have been a dinosaur. The fauna was made up of strange fat reptiles called *rhynchosaurs* which ate plants, as well as a selection of thecodontians, some of which were plant-eaters and some meat-eaters. The *thecodontians* were reptiles with strong pointed teeth and good running legs. They arose just before the beginning of the Triassic and they included the ancestors of the dinosaurs and the crocodiles. Living at the same time as the thecodontians were also many small lizard-like reptiles which ate plants or insects.

The first dinosaurs of South America, which are found in Brazil and Argentina, also lived with rhynchosaurs and thecodontians, as well as with mammal-like reptiles, so-called because they include the ancestors of the mammals.

Only one or two million years later, about 223 million years ago, the rhynchosaurs, thecodontians and mammal-like reptiles had all disappeared. The landscape was dominated by herds of large PLATEOSAURUS and medium and small dinosaurs like HALTICOSAURUS, PROCOMPSOGNATHUS and THECODONTOSAURUS. What had happened?

The evidence suggests that the rhynchosaurs, thecodontians and

▲ **The world just before the age of the dinosaurs.** A scene in north-east Scotland 225 million years ago. In the front are the curious pig-like rhynchosaurs which lived all over the world. They ate tough plants. A thecodontian, *Ornithosuchus*, is shown in the background and, in the foreground, *Saltopus*, one of the earliest dinosaurs.

mammal-like reptiles nearly all died out at about the same time. It has recently been suggested that the extinction may have been caused by changes in the climate – it became hotter and drier – and changes in plants that happened at about the same time. The dinosaurs may have been able to cope with these changes better than the other dominant reptiles. There is another theory that over a period of 30 million years the thecodontians gradually took over from the mammal-like reptiles who were in turn displaced by the dinosaurs. However the evidence does not support this idea.

Did the dinosaurs have a single ancestor? The ancestors of the dinosaurs were thecodontians, and there is growing evidence now that the dinosaurs all evolved from a single ancestor. Early forms like ISCHISAURUS and STAURIKOSAURUS are hard to classify as either prosauropods and coelurosaurs. This may be because they belonged to neither of these groups, but were primitive in all respects. Only after the rhynchosaurs and mammal-like reptiles had died out, did the major groups of dinosaurs – the coelurosaurs, the prosauropods and the ornithopods – separate out.

Dinosaur Evolution

The dinosaurs evolved for 160 million years. During this time many different forms appeared, and we have seen that they may be classified into big groups such as carnosaurs and ankylosaurs. We assume that the dinosaurs in each group are related to each other because they share common characters. We can use this information about relationships and the exact ages of each genus to make up evolutionary trees. These give suggestions about the origins and evolution of all the different groups and they can show which dinosaurs were living at any particular time.

We can see that the prosauropods and coelurosaurs were the most important dinosaurs at the end of the Triassic and beginning of the Jurassic. The sauropods replaced the prosauropods during the Jurassic, and new kinds of ornithopods evolved. In the middle and late Jurassic, stegosaurs and carnosaurs became important. During the Cretaceous, the sauropods declined, and new kinds of plant-eating dinosaurs came to dominate: the hadrosaurs, ceratopsians and ankylosaurs. Various new kinds of small meat-eating theropods also arose. These changes that occurred during the age of the dinosaurs may have been connected with changes in the plants and climates of the times. It is also likely that the new dinosaur groups had new adaptations. For example, the later ornithopods had multiple rows of grinding teeth which might have been better for dealing with tough plants than those of the sauropods.

EVOLUTION OF THE DINOSAURS

1. Coelophysis
2. Compsognathus
3. Ornithomimus
4. Deinonychus
5. Saurornithoides
6. Segnosaurus
7. Megalosaurus
8. Allosaurus
9. Tryannosaurus
10. Plateosaurus
11. Melanorosaurus
12. Cetiosaurus
13. Brachiosaurus
14. Alamosaurus
15. Heterodontosaurus
16. Camptosaurus
17. Iguanodon
18. Trachodon
19. Stegosaurus
20. Dravidosaurus
21. Hylaeosaurus
22. Ankylosaurus
23. Protoceratops
24. Triceratops

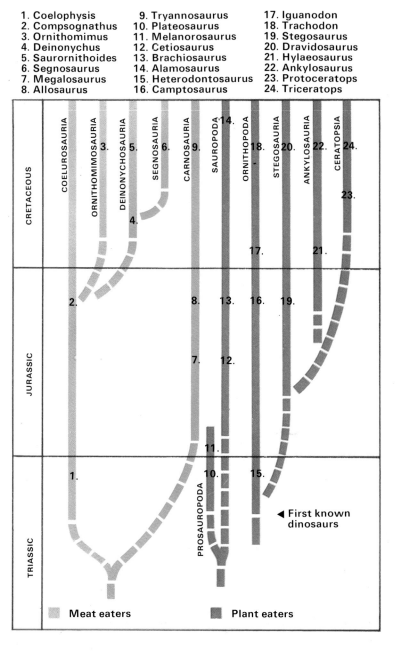

The Extinction of the Dinosaurs

Excavations of rocks from the late Cretaceous period have shown that there was a wide variety of dinosaurs living at the time. Then, at the end of the Cretaceous period, 65 million years ago, they all died out. There was no obvious slow disappearance and there were no survivors afterwards. We can guess that the dinosaurs died out at the same time everywhere in the world – although this has not been proved.

Many other kinds of animals also died out 65 million years ago, but many survived too.

We can see that nearly all the big land and sea animals died out, including the 15 or so different families of dinosaurs that were living at the end of the Cretaceous, such as STENONYCHOSAURUS, ORNITHOMIMUS, SAURORNITHOIDES, OVIRAPTOR, TYRANNOSAURUS, ALAMOSAURUS, EDMONTOSAURUS, PACHYCEPHALOSAURUS, ANKYLO-SAURUS, and TRICERATOPS.

These plants and animals died out	These plants and animals survived
forams (single-celled plankton)	most microscopic plants
some shell-fish (rudist bivalves, ammonites, belemmites)	land plants
ichthyosaurs	other shell-fish (bivalves gastropods)
plesiosaurs	snails
mosasaurs	sharks, bony fish
pterosaurs	frogs, salamanders
dinosaurs	turtles
	crocodiles
	lizards
	birds
	mammals

We can imagine how the extinction might have occurred if we look at the animals that survived. The survivors on land (frogs, turtles, lizards, birds, mammals) were mainly much smaller than the dinosaurs. Some scientists have suggested that these animals were all able to crawl into burrows or hide beneath the water to escape the calamity. However, some very big crocodiles also survived – so we should not be too hasty in choosing explanations.

At the moment scientists are trying to decide exactly how the extinctions occurred. Was it sudden or gradual? Did it happen at the same time everywhere in the world? Did some animals die out before others? As yet nobody knows the exact answers to these questions but people have thought up many different theories to explain how the dinosaurs became extinct.

Poisonous Plants or Giant Asteroid?

In the last few years, more has been written about how the dinosaurs became extinct than ever before. One explanation is that the dinosaurs could not cope with the new plants that appeared in the middle Cretaceous: the trees and flowering plants that we know today. Some scientists have suggested that these plants might have poisoned the dinosaurs, because they contained protective chemicals. It has also been thought that the new plants were less digestible or that they gave the dinosaurs constipation. These ideas are unlikely because the dinosaurs actually died out at the end of the Cretaceous period, not in the middle. They had happily eaten the new plants for 40 million years or more.

Another idea is that the mammals ate dinosaur eggs before they could hatch. They probably did sometimes, but again, the mammals had been around for a long time. In any case, it would have taken a lot of mammals to eat all the eggs. It is difficult to explain a sudden major extinction by means of this kind of argument.

One recent idea is that there were changes in the temperature world-wide. In many areas, it seems that the air and sea became hotter at the end of the Cretaceous. We have evidence for this from changes in the plants, and from the measurements of the chemical composition of certain kinds of rocks that were being laid down at the time. A rise in the temperature could have seriously upset the life of many animals, and sensitive ones might have died out. Large dinosaurs could have simply overheated.

◀ **Flowering plants** like magnolia are known near the end of the age of dinosaurs. The appearance of flowering plants probably had nothing to do with the extinction of the dinosaurs since this happened 40 million years later.

147

▲ **Early mammals** might have eaten dinosaur eggs. This did not cause their extinction since it had been happening for millions of years.

The temperature change might have had another effect. The sharp heating of the Earth's surface was followed by a gradual cooling. The dinosaurs, like TRICERATOPS and hadrosaurs, lived in a subtropical forest with tall trees and lush warm-weather plants. As the climate cooled, open pine forests spread south and brought faunas of early mammals. The extinctions might have been gradual and caused by slow climatic change over hundreds of thousands of years.

One recent explanation for the extinctions is that radiation from the Sun or from an exploding star broke through the protective layers of the Earth's atmosphere. The dinosaurs would have died from

▲ **The last dinosaurs** lived in moist subtropical forests like those of modern Florida or India. These forests changed at the same time as the dinosaurs died out.

They were followed by forests that are typical of cooler climates, like those of northern Europe or northern North America.

148

radiation sickness. One particular idea was that radiation from the Sun might have caused blindness in the dinosaurs. These are difficult ideas to prove.

The most popular 'disaster theory' for the extinction of the dinosaurs is that the Earth was hit by an *asteroid* or a comet 65 million years ago. This asteroid is thought to have weighed 4 million tonnes. When it hit the Earth it would have formed a crater 100 to 150 km wide. The asteroid would have exploded deep in the crater and shot out up to 400 million million tonnes of rock and dust. The dust would have travelled round the Earth and stayed for many months. This dust cloud would have blocked the light from the Sun. The asteroid might also have heated the air and produced acid rain. The effects of this kind of impact would be to kill off many forms of life.

No crater of the right size and age has been found. The best evidence for the asteriod is found in the sedimentary rocks at the very end of the Cretaceous. In several places around the world, at exactly 65 million years ago, geologists have found large amounts of the metal iridium in clay bands. Iridium is a rare metal which generally only comes from space. Normally we only find very small amounts which come from the tiny meteorites that land on Earth. But there are large amounts of iridium at the time the dinosaurs died out. Many scientists believe that this is good evidence for an asteroid, but others suggest that the iridium could have come from large volcanoes.

▼ **A meteorite crater** in Arizona. Some scientists think that a giant asteroid, over 10 km wide, caused the extinction of the dinosaurs. However, there is no crater of the right size or age.

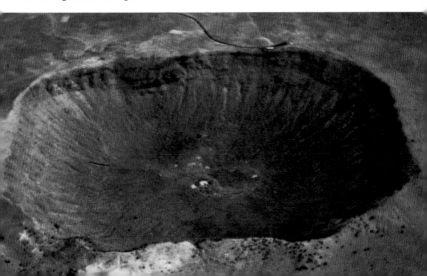

Warm-blooded Dinosaurs?

For a long time, scientists thought that dinosaurs were just big reptiles, *cold-blooded* like modern lizards and snakes. In the last ten years people have begun to wonder whether dinosaurs could have been more like mammals and birds which control their body temperatures.

In general living fishes and reptiles have the same body temperature as the water and air around them. If the air cools at night, a lizard crawls under a stone and sleeps. It cannot move around much when it is cold. When the air warms up in the morning, the lizard crawls out and basks on a rock. When it is warm enough, it can run around and hunt for food. The lizard's body temperature is controlled from outside.

The body temperature of birds and mammals is controlled from inside. They can keep their bodies warm even when the air is cold. You can test this if you feel the body of a cat or dog or bird, or a

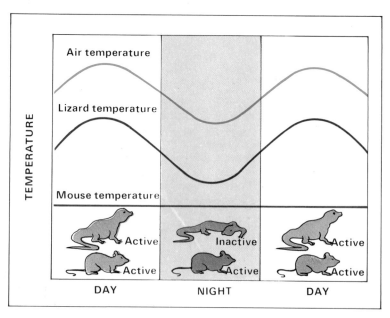

▲ **The air temperature** goes up in the daytime and down at night. Most small reptiles, like the lizard, have a similar daily pattern of body temperatures. Mammals, like the mouse, control their body temperature and it stays the same all the time.

human being, on a cold day. They can do this by burning extra food. In fact nine-tenths of what we eat is actually used to keep our body temperature the same. Put it another way; a crocodile that weighs the same as a lion eats only one-tenth of the amount of food because it does not use any to keep its body warm.

Faunas, Food and Warm-bloodedness

In any fauna the proportion of meat-eaters to plant eaters varies according to whether the meat eaters are warm- or cold-blooded. A *warm-blooded* lion eats ten times as many antelope as a cold-blooded crocodile. So a herd of antelope can provide food for ten times as many crocodiles as lions. This only tells you if the meat-eater is warm-blooded or not. It does not tell you anything about the plant-eating antelopes.

This seems a very simple idea, and we should be able to use it for fossil faunas too. If we find ten meat-eating dinosaurs for every hundred plant-eaters, we might say that the meat-eaters were cold-blooded. If we only find one meat-eater for every hundred plant-eaters, we say they were warm-blooded – of course this tells us nothing about the plant eaters. As it happens, we find very low numbers of meat-eaters in dinosaur faunas, and this is why some

▼ **One hundred antelope** can feed one lion or ten crocodiles. The lion must eat ten times as much as the crocodile eats. This is because the lion is warm-blooded and uses nine-tenths of what it eats to keep its body temperature constant.

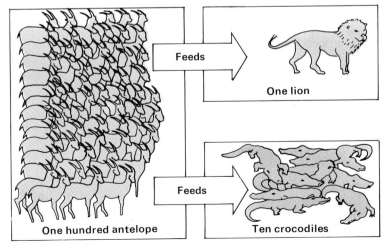

One hundred antelope   Feeds → One lion

Feeds → Ten crocodiles

people have suggested that the dinosaurs were warm-blooded just as we are.

However, we cannot be sure that this is the case. We find very big meat-eaters eat similar amounts of food whether they control their temperature from inside or outside. There are also some plant-eaters which are protected by their size. Elephants are hardly ever attacked by lions or tigers – they are just too big. Maybe APATOSAURUS was also safe from attack from ALLOSAURUS because it was so huge. This means that we should not include the numbers of *Apatosaurus* in any calculations – they were not part of what *Allosaurus* would eat. So calculations of this sort cannot tell us for sure whether dinosaurs were warm-blooded or not.

Bone Structure

The other main evidence for warm-blooded dinosaurs has been the bone structure. Most living reptiles have slow-growing bone. Under a microscope, a section of reptile bone will appear solid with noticeable rings. These rings are laid down every year – they are rather like the growth rings in a tree. Living mammals have fast-growing bone with lots of canals for blood vessels. These canals pass right through the bone and allow the blood to flow easily – remember that bone is a living structure just like other parts of the body. In mammals the blood carries minerals to and from the bone, and this allows rapid growth when the animals are young. Dinosaur bone looks exactly like the bone of a cow. Does this mean that dinosaurs also had inside temperature control?

Once again we cannot prove it. Only large mammals and birds have lots of canals in their bone. Small mammals and birds have rather solid bone like crocodiles and sea turtles have bone with canals. So, lots of canals in the bone seems to indicate large size – and we already know that the dinosaurs were big!

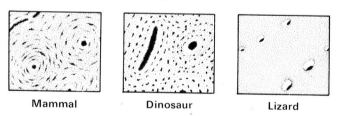

Mammal   Dinosaur   Lizard

Dinosaurs: a Special Case

Although we cannot prove that dinosaurs were warm-blooded in the way that mammals are today, it does seem that they were different from modern reptiles. Most scientists have agreed that it is likely that

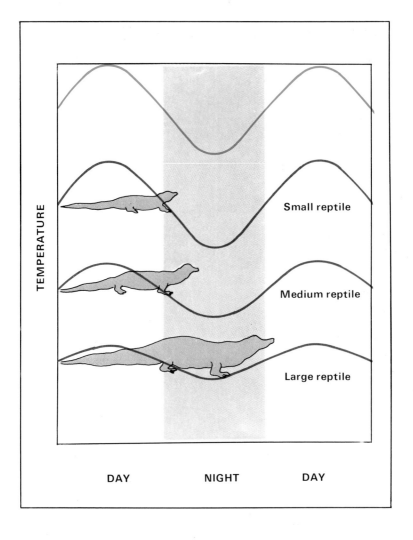

DAY   NIGHT   DAY

the small and medium two-legged dinosaurs, like DEINONYCHUS, DROMAEOSAURUS and OVIRAPTOR were warm-blooded with some inside control of body temperature. How could this be? Scientists need to study fossil bone in more detail before they can say what the different structures mean.

Scientists have studied crocodiles and alligators of different sizes and they have discovered something very important. The bigger animals had far more constant body temperatures than the small ones just because of their large size. The body temperatures of small crocodiles followed the air temperature as it dropped during the night and rose during the day. In bigger crocodiles, the body took longer to cool down at night and longer to heat up in the daytime. This is simply because of insulation. The hot water tank in your home is wrapped up in layers of foam to keep the heat in. In just the same way, the big crocodiles are wrapped up in thick layers of flesh and fat and these also keep the heat in. Just imagine how well insulated a big dinosaur would be!

So, the big dinosaurs were warm-blooded, but not in the way that we are – it happened as a by-product of their large size. Also, nine-tenths of their food did not have to be used to keep their body temperatures constant. Look at the picture of APATOSAURUS or DIPLODOCUS and look at the size of its mouth. Think how difficult it would be for *Apatosaurus* to eat ten times its ordinary amount of food to control its body temperature from inside.

Standing, Walking, and Running

Dinosaurs had their legs tucked under the body – they stood upright like a horse or an elephant. Most living reptiles have sprawling legs which stick out sideways and their stomachs rest on the ground. In mammals and birds, the feet and knees or elbows are right under the body and they can hold up a heavy animal. Big turtles and crocodiles can raise themselves up by partly tucking their legs underneath their bodies if they want to run. But the big dinosaurs were too heavy for this kind of system.

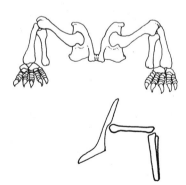

◀ **Sprawling legs.** Most reptiles stand in this way with the legs pointing sideways. Animals that sprawl cannot be very heavy, and they cannot run very fast.

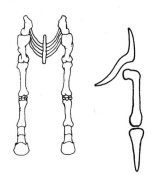

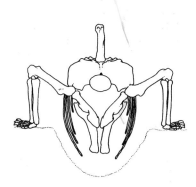

▲ **Upright legs.** Most living mammals and birds have their legs tucked under their bodies, as did the dinosaurs. This allows them to be big and to run fast.

Diplodocus Sprawler

An old reconstruction of DIPLO-DOCUS showed it with its legs out sideways like a lizard and its stomach dragging on the ground. A dinosaur expert at the time proved that this was impossible because the leg bones could not fit together in that arrangement. Also, the stomach would not have rested on the ground, but it would have been a metre or two lower than the soles of the feet. *Diplodocus* could only have walked as a sprawler if it had its stomach in a trench in the ground!

Several facts show that dinosaurs stood upright. First of all, the shape of the pelvis and leg bones is quite clear. The head of the thigh bone is bent inwards and the hip bones have a saucer-shaped socket for it which points sideways and downwards. In a sprawler, the head of the thigh bone is not bent inwards, and the hip bone socket only points sideways.

We can also look at the fossilized trackways made by dinosaurs. In these, the two lines of footprints made by the left and right feet are close together. A sprawler makes two lines of footprints that are far apart.

▲ **An old idea** about *Diplodocus* as a sprawler. Its leg bones show that this is impossible, and its body was so deep that its stomach would have been below its feet!

▲ **A trackway** of *Megalosaurus* footprints. Fossil footprints are often poorly preserved, but the size of the animal can be seen. Its walking speed can be worked out from the stride length.

Running Speeds

We can learn more from fossilized footprints. These often show the shape and size of the animal that made them. We can count the toes, and even see claw marks sometimes. If we measure the distance between two prints made by the same foot (the stride length), and if we know the size of the animal that made the tracks, it is easy to work out how fast it was moving. The faster an animal runs, the further apart its footprints become. Try walking slowly, quickly and running on a beach or in the snow and see how far apart your footprints are when you run.

These simple sums have shown that dinosaurs walked at speeds of 4–20 kilometres per hour, depending on size. Small coelurosaurs walked at 4–13 kilometres per hour, and sauropods at 15–20 kilometres per hour. The fastest running speed worked out so far is 56 kilometres per hour for the coelurosaur GALLIMIMUS. Of course, we can only measure the speeds we see in the fossilized footprints. These might show slower speeds more often than fast ones. The giant sauropods could not have run as fast as *Gallimimus*. Their bodies were too heavy, and the bones of the legs would have been under great strain at high speed. APATOSAURUS could have reached a speed of 12 kilometres per hour. A human being runs at speeds of up to 24 or 25 kilometres per hour (but only for short distances!)

Some interesting trackways show how dinosaurs swam. A trackway of *Apatosaurus* made under water shows only the marks of its front feet. Unless the animal was performing a very difficult trick by balancing on its arms, we must guess that it was floating in a lake. It used its front legs to push itself along by shoving against the muddy bottom. Another trackway, recently found in Connecticut shows just a few scratch marks made by the claws of a carnosaur like MEGALOSAURUS. Again, the dinosaur might have been hopping along on its toenails like a ballet dancer. Or, more likely, we guess that it was floating and just pushing itself along with a few thrusts of its toes on the bottom.

How Dinosaurs Lived

Migrating Herds

Dinosaur footprints show that at least some dinosaurs travelled in herds. Scientists have found huge surfaces of mudstone just covered with dinosaur footprints. Sometimes several rows of footprints made by different animals are all going in the same direction. There may be big ones on the outside and smaller ones between.

Could it be that herds of dinosaurs like ANCHISAURUS, IGUANODON and ANATOSAURUS travelled together? It has been suggested that herds of big dinosaurs migrated for long distances in search of fresh pastures. Today we can observe antelope or elephant migrating during the dry season in Africa. Could it also be that young dinosaurs travelled in the middle for protection?

A HERD OF TRICERATOPS

Dinosaur Eggs

As far as we know, young dinosaurs hatched out of eggs as is the case in most living reptiles. Many dinosaur eggs have been discovered, and some of them have small skeletons inside. The eggs could be round or 'egg-shaped' or long and thin rather like a sausage. Scientists have not only found single eggs. They have also discovered nests, some containing 10 eggs or more.

The most important thing about dinosaur eggs is that they were never very big. Small and medium dinosaurs had eggs the size of a hen's egg or a turkey's egg, or just a little bigger. PROTOCERATOPS, which was 2 metres long, had sausage-shaped eggs just over 20 centimetres long and with a 1-millimetre-thick shell. If dinosaur eggs were the same proportions for the bigger sauropods, BRACHIOSAURUS would have had an egg that was 2.5 metres long. However, the biggest dinosaur eggs known, which were probably laid by the 12-metre-long sauropod HYPSELOSAURUS, were only 25–30 centimetres long and had an eggshell 2.6 millimetres thick. This is probably the biggest size any dinosaur egg ever reached. The largest egg of any living animal is that of the ostrich which is usually about 15 centimetres long. The reason

▼ **A nest** of the eggs of *Protoceratops*. The eggs are 20 cm long, and they were laid in a circle, all pointing outwards.

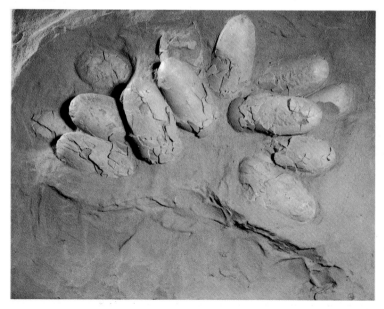

why sauropods and other big dinosaurs did not lay bigger eggs is simple. Big eggs need thick eggshells or they would collapse. A very big dinosaur egg would have had such a thick shell that the baby dinosaur would never have managed to break its way out!

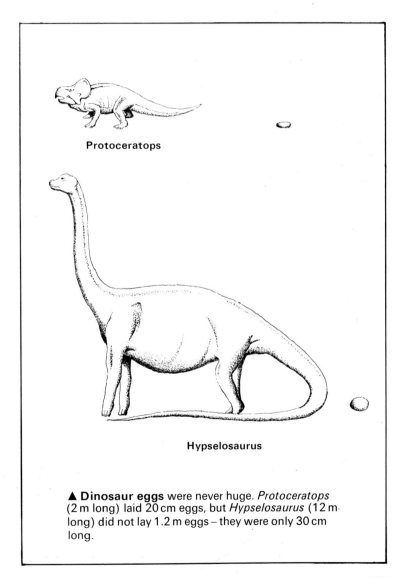

Protoceratops

Hypselosaurus

▲ **Dinosaur eggs** were never huge. *Protoceratops* (2 m long) laid 20 cm eggs, but *Hypselosaurus* (12 m long) did not lay 1.2 m eggs – they were only 30 cm long.

Babies and Nests

In 1978 some very well preserved baby dinosaurs were discovered. A whole nest of 15 young hadrosaurs was found in Montana, USA in 1978. The young animals were about 1 metre long, and their mother was 7–9 metres long. They were named MAIASAURA (see the dictionary). They were all found in a fossilized nest which was 2 metres wide and 0.75 metres deep. Broken eggshells lay around. The nest was surrounded by a mound of soil and it seems to have been built specially to protect the eggs. The discoverers of this nest thought that it suggested that the young dinosaurs were cared for by their parents after they hatched out. A few years later, the same collectors found several more nests nearby. This suggested that the dinosaurs made their nests close together and that the mothers returned year after year to the same spot to lay their eggs.

▼ **A nest** of the duck-billed dinosaur *Maiasaura*. The eggs were laid in a circular pattern in a high mound of earth.

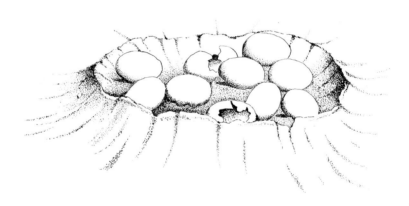

In the 1920s some nests of PROTOCERATOPS eggs were found in Mongolia. The eggs were arranged in a simple pattern, all pointing outwards. It seems that the mother dug a bowl-shaped hole and laid the eggs in a circle. There were often several layers of eggs too. Then the mother would have covered the eggs with earth to protect them until the babies hatched out. Babies, juveniles and adults of *Protoceratops* are often found together, which suggests that they also lived in a family group.

160

Dinosaur diets

What did all the different dinosaurs eat and how do we know anyway? We can tell a lot by looking at their teeth. The carnosaurs like TYRANNOSAURUS and MEGALOSAURUS had huge pointed teeth shaped rather like scimitars. This shows that they killed animals and tore up the meat for food. Their teeth had zig-zag spikes along the cutting edges, like steak-knives.

Most other dinosaurs ate plants. The sauropods had broad flat spoon-shaped teeth, sometimes with a slight point. The ornithopods and armoured dinosaurs had similar flat leaf-shaped teeth, sometimes with various ridges and extra grinding surfaces. The exact arrangement of the teeth tells us the kinds of plants they ate. For example, the duck-billed dinosaurs had rows and rows of tightly packed teeth in each jaw – maybe up to 2000

▲ **The tooth** of a meat-eating dinosaur. The tooth had a zig-zag cutting edge, just like a steak knife.

teeth! These provided a huge grinding and chopping surface for smashing and breaking up tough plants.

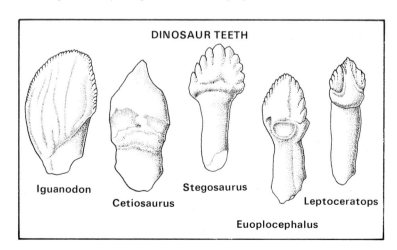

DINOSAUR TEETH

Iguanodon

Cetiosaurus

Stegosaurus

Leptoceratops

Euoplocephalus

161

Jaws and Stomach Stones

The various types of teeth provide us with some idea of what the different dinosaurs ate, and we can learn more about dinosaur diets by looking at the bones of the jaws. The patterns on the bone surfaces and the arrangement of the bones shows us how the jaw muscles were arranged. So we can reconstruct the muscles on the head of a hadrosaur and see that it could pull its jaws shut strongly enough to break branches off a tree. We can also work out that it pulled its lower jaw back and forwards to chop up its food. However, it could not move its jaws sideways as we can. You can try moving your jaw back and forwards and sideways. We need these movements to grind up our food before we swallow it. Dinosaurs must have had to swallow their food in large chunks!

If we try to decide what a particular dinosaur could eat, we should obviously find out what plants and animals were around at the time. So, APATOSAURUS could have eaten various kinds of ferns, tree ferns and conifers, but not flowers or deciduous trees since they did not exist. Sometimes, we are very lucky and find some direct evidence of

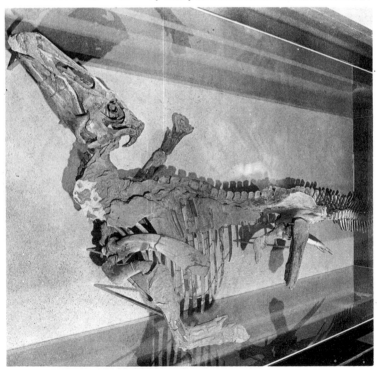

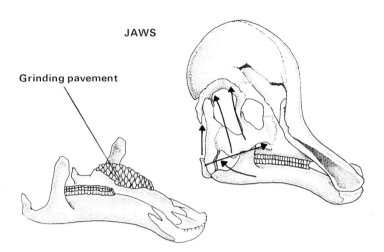

JAWS

Grinding pavement

▲ **The lower jaw** of a duck-billed dinosaur. There were many rows of ridged teeth which fitted together tightly. Some duck-bills had as many as 2000 teeth. They used them to chop up tough plants, but they could not chew from side to side.

▲ **The main lines** of the jaw muscles of a duck-billed dinosaur. We can work out where the muscles attached by looking at the jaw bones. We can also work out how strong each muscle was, and then work out how the jaws worked.

dinosaur diet. One or two mummified duck-bills have been found with remains of pine needles, twigs and pine cones in their stomachs!

Another source of evidence about how dinosaurs ate is gastroliths, or stomach stones. These are polished pebbles that

◀ **The mummified body** of a dinosaur. The duck-billed dinosaur *Anatosaurus* has been found in Alberta, Canada, with all the bones of the skeleton, as well as remains of skin and dried up tendons. Some of the mummified bodies also have stomach contents, and these show that *Anatosaurus* ate pine needles.

are found in the stomach area. Today, chickens and other birds swallow grit to help grind up their food in their guts (birds have no teeth to do this). Several living reptiles such as crocodiles also swallow stones for this reason, and it may have been a way that dinosaurs avoided getting indigestion from swallowing unchewed food.

From time to time dinosaur skeletons have been found with the remains of another animal inside. Sometimes these prove to be unborn young but in some cases they are the remains of the dinosaur's last meal.

163

Clubs, Claws and Spikes

We can learn a lot about how dinosaurs behaved by comparing some of their claws, horns, spikes, clubs and other weapons with living animals. We have already noticed the fearsome teeth of the carnosaurs. Many of them also had vicious claws on their hands and feet to attack with. These claws were like sickles and could be 30 centimetres or more long in some forms. MEGALOSAURUS and ALLOSAURUS could use their hands, and DEINONYCHUS its feet to slash at other dinosaurs. They might have tried to grasp them by the neck using teeth and claws, or they might have tried to cut their bodies open with fierce kicks.

Many of the herbivores were protected in some way. IGUANODON had a spike on its thumb. The three groups of 'armoured' dinosaurs had an impressive selection of defensive weapons. The ankylosaurs had clubs at the ends of their tails made from heavy knobs of bone. If any ankylosaur was attacked, it probably stopped moving, crouched down and swung its tail. Most ankylosaurs were protected on top by bone plates under the skin and a frill of spikes round the edge of the body.

The stegosaurs, such as STEGOSAURUS and KENTROSAURUS, had various plates and spines along their backs. These stuck up in the air and out sideways. If a

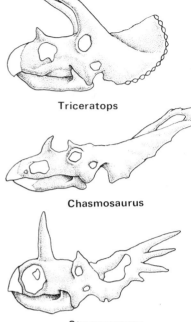

Triceratops

Chasmosaurus

Styracosaurus

stegosaur kept moving, a meat-eater could not get in near enough to seize its prey; and the stegosaurs could swing their spiked tails around too. The ceratopsians had heavy bony frills on the backs of their heads which protected the delicate neck. There were often horns on the head to help with protection. There was a great range of ceratopsian frills, and these are used to identify the different species.

PACHYCEPHALOSAURUS had a very thick bony head. It has been suggested that male animals butted each other in ritual fights to win females. This kind of behaviour is seen among living deer, sheep and antelope.

Horns, Crests and Frills

Some of the amazing dinosaur heads that we have seen may have been for display – rather like the colourful feather patterns in different kinds of birds. The horns and frills may have allowed dinosaurs to recognise members of their own species. The best example is the hadrosaurs. Many of these 'duck-bills' had large growths of bone on top of their heads, shaped like flat plates, long tubes, pillars and helmets. Some of them had no crests at all. In their skeletons the hadrosaurs are often very similar, but we can tell them apart by their head crests. The hadrosaurs may have used the crests for the same thing.

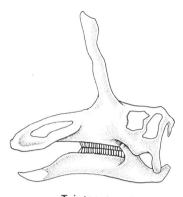

Tsintaosaurus

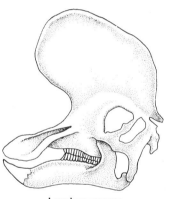

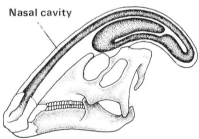

Nasal cavity

Parasaurolophus

Lambeosaurus

We can take this idea a bit further with the hadrosaurs. It turns out that the crests were made largely from the nasal bones. The breathing tubes ran up inside the crest and back down into the mouth. If the hadrosaur breathed out through its nose it would have made a loud and deep honking noise. The different hadrosaurs had different patterns of breathing tubes in their crests and we can compare these with different kinds of musical instruments. So, each species of hadrosaur probably made a different honk, toot or whistle. These may have helped the hadrosaurs to recognise other members of their own species. They might also have bellowed and honked at each other as a threat or display.

165

Record Breakers

Record breakers
The dinosaurs include the biggest land animals of all time. In this section, some estimates for record-breaking dinosaurs of all kinds are given. Remember that many of the numbers are *estimates*, and they may be altered by new information.

The longest dinosaurs
Brachiosaurus (23–27 metres)
Diplodocus (27 metres)
Antarctosaurus (30 metres)
'*Supersaurus*' (?24–30 metres: not well known yet)
'*Ultrasaurus*' (?30–35 metres: even less well known)

The tallest dinosaurs
Brachiosaurus (12 metres)
'*Supersaurus*' (?15 metres)
'*Ultrasaurus*' (?16–17 metres)

The widest dinosaur
Ankylosaurus (5 metres)

The heaviest dinosaurs
Brachiosaurus (78 tonnes)
Antarctosaurus (80 tonnes)
'*Supersaurus*' (?75–100 tonnes)
'*Ultrasaurus*' (?100–140 tonnes)

1. Ultrasaurus
2. Supersaurus
3. Brachiosaurus

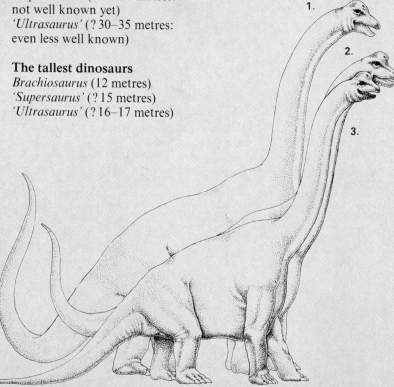

1.
2.
3.

Pigeon

Psittacosaurus

The smallest dinosaurs
Psittacosaurus baby (23–25 centimetres long)
Mussaurus baby (about 25 centimetres long)
Saltopus adult (60 centimetres long; weight: ?900 g)
Compsognathus adult (75–91 centimetres long; weight: ?3 kilogrammes)

The oldest known dinosaur
Staurikosaurus from the late Triassic of Brazil (about 225 million years old)

The first dinosaur fossil found
Megalosaurus thigh bone found near Oxford, England in 1677

The fastest dinosaurs
Unknown Cretaceous carnosaur: 43 kilometres per hour (from a fossil trackway)
Gallimimus: 56 kilometres per hour (from the shape of its legs)

The first dinosaur named
Megalosaurus (1824)

The largest number of dinosaurs found together
over 100 skeletons of *Coelophysis* collected in 1947 at Ghost Ranch, New Mexico, USA

The brainiest dinosaur
Stenonychosaurus

The most stupid dinosaur
Diplodocus (it had the smallest brain relative to its body size)

The biggest dinosaur egg
Hypselosaurus egg (30 centimetres long; capacity: about 2 litres)

Things to do

Dinosaur fossils are not very easy to find. Even if you were lucky enough to find one, it would be a bit too big to take home! However, it is very easy to collect fossils of plants, shells and other animals that lived with the dinosaurs, or at other times in the Earth's history. How do you set about collecting fossils?

You will have to find out where to look first. Ask your local library or museum, or ask a science teacher at school for advice. There are many books about the geology and fossils of different areas, and you should try to find one about yours. This will tell you the kinds of rocks and the kinds of fossils that may be found nearby.

After you have found out where to go and what to look for, you will need to make up a fossil hunter's kit. This is made up as follows:

(1) Heavy shoes or wellington boots.
(2) A hammer with a sharp end, or a small pick, or a hammer and cold chisel.
(3) A notebook and pencil.
(4) An old paintbrush and tooth brush.
(5) Lots of plastic bags and old newspapers.
(6) Small tins or boxes.
(7) A collecting bag.

▶ **A fossil collector's kit.** These are some of the things you may need to collect fossils: pick hammers, heavy hammers and chisels, scrapers, newspaper, string and boxes to put the fossils in, a notebook and pencil to write down where you found your fossils, a rucksack to carry them in, and a magnifying glass to look at small specimens.

▲ **This is the kind of place** to look for fossils. The sedimentary rocks are broken down by the sea, and new fossils keep appearing.

You need the hammer to break open pieces of stone, and the brushes to clean off loose dirt. If you find a fossil you put it into a bag, or wrap it up in newspaper. You must write down in your notebook where you find your fossils so that you don't forget.

There are some important things to remember about fossil hunting. Most fossils are found in mudstones or limestones, so these are the best places to look.

Also, fossils are usually found in large numbers at particular levels. So, it is best to look around a place first before you start hammering. You may see loose pieces of stone with fossils lying around. Try to find exactly

WARNING! Be very careful if you collect fossils on beaches and in quarries. These are dangerous places. Always ask for permission, and keep away from all high cliffs and quarry walls.

169

where they have come from, and hammer there. Finally, and this is very important, be very careful. Most fossil sites are under cliffs or in quarries, and these are dangerous places. Keep away from any loose rock, and don't go into a quarry that is working. Always ask for permission to cross fields or to go into old quarries.

Making a Museum

When you bring your fossils home, you might want to clean them up. If they are quite hard, you can use water and a brush. You can also pick off the rock with an old penknife or a needle (an old hat pin or a probe) – but be careful not to damage the fossil, or yourself! Then you must write a label for the fossil. This should say where you found it (the name of the quarry or nearest building, and details of which bed it came from – for example 'the grey 1-metre-thick limestone bed, 3 metres above the bottom of the quarry'), what the fossil is, and how old it is. You can find out this information if you ask in your local museum or library. You can store fossils in cardboard trays made from small boxes, in drawers or on shelves. After a while, you will have a museum of your own to show to your friends. Most geologists and palaeontologists started off by collecting fossils when they were young.

Scenes of Ancient Life

You can collect plastic models of dinosaurs and reconstruct how they lived for yourself. You can buy these models in many toy shops and in museum shops. Lots of the small soft plastic dinosaurs are not very accurate – they have huge mouths with lots of teeth. Look for the better life-like models: museum shops usually sell these. You can also buy plastic kits to make your own dinosaur models and you can paint them whatever colours you like.

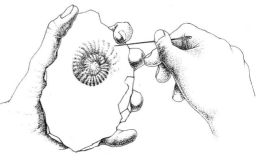

▶ **Cleaning up a fossil.** You can use any needle or small probe to scrape or poke the rock from your fossils. Always scrape away from the fossil to avoid damaging it. Also, scrape away from yourself as a safety precaution.

▶ Your fossil museum. You can keep fossils in drawers, or boxes. Clean each fossil, and write down exactly where each one comes from. If you have found out what the fossil is, write that down too.

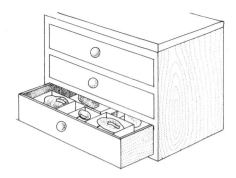

When you have a collection of model dinosaurs, you can sort them out into their different geological ages using this book: late Triassic, late Jurassic and so on. Then you can look at scenes of these different ages in this book and in other dinosaur books, and see what kinds of plants and animals were living at the time. Copy some of these scenes on to white cardboard and make a background for each set of dinosaur models. This will give you the best idea of what the world was like during the age of the dinosaurs.

▲ **The Prehistoric Park,** Calgary, Canada. Models of dinosaurs are set in a landscape.

Collecting Stamps

You can learn about the dinosaurs of the world by collecting stamps. Many countries have produced postage stamps with prehistoric animals on them, and this makes a fascinating theme to collect. You will find colourful sets produced by Poland (below) and San Marino, as well as odd stamps from countries as far apart as the United States, Mongolia and China. You can obtain more information from stamp dealers and stamp magazines.

Museums

All the dinosaurs that you have read about in this book are kept in museums around the world. Museums that have dinosaur have displays of their best specimens: usually whole skeletons and skulls. Some of the most important dinosaur museums in the world are listed on pages 174–5, and you should try to visit one of them if you can. There are also dramatic outdoor displays of model dinosaurs, such as the life-size reconstructions of dinosaurs and other prehistoric animals in the Crystal Palace Park in London. These are the models made in the 19th century by Waterhouse Hawkins, following Richard Owen's specifications. They are not all scientifically accurate, but they show how people at that time imagined dinosaurs to look. In Canada there is a much more up-to-date display at the Prehistoric Park in Calgary, which opened in 1983. The park itself is divided into different areas which were specially designed to display scaled-down

▼ **One of the best dinosaurs in a museum.** A skeleton of *Brachiosaurus* in the Humboldt Museum, Berlin, East Germany. This huge skeleton nearly fills a large room that was built for it.

portions of Western Canada as they may have appeared during the Mesozoic Era. There are hundreds of other museums with dinosaurs on display, so try your local museum too.

Museums Worldwide

ARGENTINA
La Plata: La Plata Museum

AUSTRALIA
Fortitude Valley, Queensland: Queensland Musem

BELGIUM
Brussels: Royal Institute of Natural Sciences

CANADA
Calgary, Alberta: Zoological Gardens
Drumheller, Alberta: Tyrrell Museum of Palaeontology
Edmonton, Alberta: Provincial Museum of Alberta
Ottawa, Ontario: National Museum of Natural Sciences
Patricia, Alberta: Dinosaur Provincial Park (another working
    display. A huge area of badlands – an area rich in fossil
    deposits – with dinosaurs being excavated).
Toronto, Ontario: Royal Ontario Museum

CHINA
Beijing: Beijing Natural History Museum

FRANCE
Paris: National Museum of Natural History

GERMANY (EAST)
East Berlin: Institute of Natural History and Humboldt University
    Museum

GERMANY (WEST)
Frankfurt-am-Maine: Senckenburg Museum
Stuttgart: State Museum for Natural History
Tübingen: Institute and Museum of Geology and Palaeontology

INDIA
Calcutta: Geology Museum, Indian Statistical Institute

JAPAN
Tokyo: National Science Museum

MONGOLIA
Ulan-Bator: State Central Museum

NIGER
Niamey: National Museum

SOUTH AFRICA
Cape Town: South African Museum

UK
Belfast: Ulster Museum
Cambridge: Sedgwick Museum
Edinburgh: Royal Museum of Scotland
Leicester: Leicestershire Museums
London: British Museum (Natural History)
Maidstone: Maidstone Museum
Oxford: University Museum
Sandown, Isle of Wight: Museum of Isle of Wight Geology

USA
Cambridge, Massachusetts: Museum of Comparative Zoology, Harvard Museum
Chicago, Illinois: Field Museum of Natural History
Denver, Colorado: Denver Museum of Natural History
Jensen, Utah: Dinosaur National Monument (a working display of a late Jurassic bone bed with lots of giant dinosaur skeletons lying as they were found)
Los Angeles, California: Los Angeles County Museum of Natural History
New Haven, Connecticut: Peabody Museum of Natural History, Yale University
New York City, New York: American Museum of Natural History
Princeton, New Jersey: Museum of Natural History, Princeton University
Salt Lake City, Utah: Utah Museum of Natural History
Washington DC: National Museum of Natural History, Smithsonian Insitute

USSR
Leningrad: Central Geological and Prospecting Museum
Moscow: Palaeontological Museum

Classification Table

Order ORNITHISCHIA

Suborder STEGOSAURIA
Dacentrurus, Dravidosaurus, Kentrosaurus, Lexovisaurus, Scelidosaurus, Stegosaurus.

Suborder ANKYLOSAURIA
Acanthopholis, Ankylosaurus, Dyoplosaurus, Hylaeosaurus, Nodosaurus, Panoplosaurus, Pinacosaurus, Silvisaurus, Struthiosaurus.

Suborder CERATOPSIA
Anchiceratops, Bagaceratops, Brachyceratops, Chasmosaurus, Leptoceratops, Microceratops, Monoclonius, Pachyrhinosaurus, Pentaceratops, Protoceratops, Psittacosaurus, Styracosaurus, Torosaurus, Triceratops.

Suborder ORNITHOPODA
Anatosaurus, Brachylophosaurus, Camptosaurus, Claosaurus, Corythosaurus, Dryosaurus, Edmontosaurus, Fabrosaurus, Geranosaurus, Hadrosaurus, Heterodontosaurus, Hypacrosaurus, Hypsilophodon, Iguanodon, Lambeosaurus, Lycorhinus, Maiasaura, Muttaburrasaurus, Othnielia, Ouranosaurus, Parasaurolophus, Parksosaurus, Prosaurolophus, Saurolophus, Scutellosaurus, Secernosaurus, Shantungosaurus, Troödon, Tsintaosaurus, Zephyrosaurus.

Order SAURISCHIA

Suborder THEROPODA
Infraorder COELUROSAURIA
Coelophysis, Coelurus, Compsognathus, Halticosaurus, Ornitholestes, Procompsognathus, Saltopus, ?Segisaurus, Syntarsus.

Infraorder ORNITHOMIMOSAURIA
?Avimimus, Elaphrosaurus, Gallimimus, Ornithomimus, ?Oviraptor, Struthiomimus.

Infraorder DEINONYCHOSAURIA
Deinocheirus, Deinonychus, Dromaeosaurus, ?Itemirus, ?Noasaurus, Saurornithoides, Stenonychosaurus, ?Therizinosaurus, ?Velociraptor.

Infraorder SEGNOSAURIA
Segnosaurus

Infraorder CARNOSAURIA
Acrocanthosaurus, Albertosaurus, Allosaurus, Carcharodontosaurus, Ceratosaurus, Daspletosaurus, Dilophosaurus, Dryptosaurus, Megalosaurus, Spinosaurus, Tarbosaurus, Tyrannosaurus.

Suborder
SAUROPODAMORPHA
Infraorder PROSAUROPODA
*Ammosaurus, Anchisaurus,
Euskelosaurus, ?Ischisaurus,
Lufengosaurus, Massospondylus,
Melanorosaurus, ?Mussaurus,
Plateosaurus, ?Staurikosaurus,
Thecodontosaurus,
?Vulcanodon.*

Infraorder SAUROPODA
*Alamosaurus, Antarctosaurus,
Apatosaurus, Barapsaurus,
Barosaurus, Brachiosaurus,
Camarasaurus, Cetiosaurus,
Dicraeosaurus, Diplodocus,
Euhelopus, Hypselosaurus,
Mamenchisaurus,
Nemegtosaurus,
Opisthocoelicaudia,
Pelorosaurus, Rhoetosaurus,
Saltasaurus, 'Supersaurus',
Titanosaurus, 'Ultrasaurus'.*

Books to Read

You will find books about
dinosaurs, fossils and evolution
in your local library and
bookshop. Some good recent
books are listed here.

Dinosaurs
Collins Guide to Dinosaurs by
David Lambert (Collins, 1983)
Dinosaurs by L. B. Halstead
(Blandford, 1981)
Dinosaurs by David Lambert
(Kingfisher Books, 1978)
A New Look at the Dinosaurs by
A. J. Charig (Heinemann, 1979)
*Do You Know? How Dinosaurs
Lived* by M. J. Benton (Piccolo,
1985)
Dinosaurs, an Illustrated History
by E. H. Colbert (Hammond,
1983)
*The Illustrated Encyclopedia of
Dinosaurs* by D. B. Norman
(Salamander, 1985)
*The Evolution and Ecology of
the Dinosaurs* by L. B. Halstead
(Peter Lowe, 1975)

Fossils
Fossils by Richard Fortey
(Heinemann, 1982)
Hunting the Past by L. B.
Halstead (Hamish Hamilton,
1982)
Fossils and Fossil Collecting by
Roger Hamilton (Hamlyn, 1975)
The Story of Life on Earth by
M. J. Benton (Kingfisher
Books, 1986)

Evolution
Life on Earth by David
Attenborough (Collins, 1979)
Evolution by Colin Patterson
(Heinemann, 1978)
*The New Evolutionary Time-
table* by S. M. Stanley (Basic
Books, 1981)

Clubs and Societies
In certain towns there are
geology clubs which organise
lectures and field trips to collect
rocks and fossils. Ask at your
local library for information
about these.

177

Glossary

Ankylosaur An armoured dinosaur which has a covering of bony plates on its back and a knobbly tail. See Ankylosauria in the dictionary.

Armoured dinosaur There were three groups of armoured dinosaurs which were protected by coverings of bony plates, spikes or horns. See Ankylosauria, Ceratopsia and Stegosauria in the dictionary.

Carnosaur A large meat-eating dinosaur. See Carnosauria in the dictionary.

Carnosaur
(Allosaurus)

Ceratopsian An armoured dinosaur with horns on its snout and face, and a bony frill over its neck. See Ceratopsia in the dictionary.

Classification The sorting of animals and plants into an order that shows how they are related to each other.

Clubmoss A plant related to the fern. Its name derives from the club-shaped spike where the spores are carried.

Coelurosaur A small meat-eating dinosaur. See Coelurosauria in the dictionary.

Cold-blooded An animal, like a reptile, amphibian or fish, which cannot control its body to a constant temperature as we can.

Cretaceous The third geological period in the 'age of dinosaurs', the time from 140 to 65 million years ago.

Cycad A plant with a thick, unbranched trunk and long fern-like leaves. In the Mesozoic Era cycads were sometimes tall, like trees but modern cycads are only a few feet high.

Deinonychosaur A medium-sized meat-eating dinosaur that had a huge claw on its foot. See Deinonychosauria in the dictionary.

Duck-billed dinosaur Another name for a hadrosaur, a kind of two-legged plant-eater that had a broad beak-like snout.

Era A long section of geological time, such as the Mesozoic Era.

Evolution The development of plants and animals through geological time, and the way that this development comes about. Animals and plants *evolve* or change as a result of changes in their living conditions and *natural selection*.

Extinction The death of a group of plants or animals. We usually think about sudden extinctions, such as when the dinosaurs died out, or became *extinct*, at the same time.

Family A group of closely related plants or animals.

Iguanodon hand

Fauna A collection of animals that all live, or lived, together in the same place at the same time.

Formation A division of the historical record of the rocks.

Fossil The remains of something that once lived. Fossils are often millions of years old, and turned to stone, but not always. Dinosaurs are known only from fossils. Fossils are made by the process of fossilization.

Ceratopsian
(Styracosaurus)

Genus A group of very closely related species of plants or animals. We say, one *genus*, two *genera*.

Habitat The surroundings in which an animal lives. This includes the climate, temperature, altitude, amount of water, plants and so on.

Hadrosaur A duck-billed dinosaur; a kind of plant-eating dinosaur that had a broad flat snout.

Ichthyosaur A fish-reptile that was shaped like a dolphin and lived in the seas at the same time as the dinosaurs roamed the land.

Jurassic The second geological period in the 'age of dinosaurs'; the time from 205 to 140 million years ago.

Mammal An animal with hair that feeds its young with milk, such as a mouse, a rabbit, a cat, a dog, a horse, an elephant.

HADROSAURS

Parasaurolophus

Mammal-like reptile A primitive kind of reptile that lived before the dinosaurs and was related to the ancestors of the mammals.

Mesozoic The 'age of the dinosaurs', the time from 245 to 65 million years ago which includes the Triassic, Jurassic and Cretaceous periods.

Natural selection The main process of evolution, in which the animals that are best adapted to find food and to escape from meat-eaters end up by producing the most young: 'survival of the fittest'.

Order A large group of species that are rather distantly related to each other – larger than a *genus* or family.

Ornithischian A 'bird-hipped' dinosaur. This big group of dinosaurs includes all of the two-legged plant-eaters, and all of the armoured dinosaurs. See Ornithischia in the dictionary.

Edmontosaurus

Corythosaurus

Saurolophus

**Ornithopod
(Iguanodon)**

Reconstruction A model or drawing that shows what a dinosaur may have looked like.

Reptile A cold-blooded scaly four-legged animal that lays eggs on land. Living reptiles are lizards, snakes, turtles and crocodiles.

Rhynchosaur A pig-like plant-eating reptile with a beaked snout that lived just before the dinosaurs.

Saurischian A 'lizard-hipped' dinosaur – one of the meat-eaters or large four-legged plant-eating dinosaurs. See Saurischia in the dictionary.

Ornithopod A two legged plant-eater. See Ornithopoda in the dictionary.

Palaeontologist A scientist who studies fossils.

Period A division of geological times, such as the Triassic, Jurassic or Cretaceous.

Plesiosaur A large fish-eating reptile that had a long neck and swam with paddles. The plesiosaurs lived in the seas in the age of the dinosaurs.

Radioactivity The breakdown of chemical elements into different elements and giving off energy. Radioactivity can give an idea of geological age.

Oviraptor

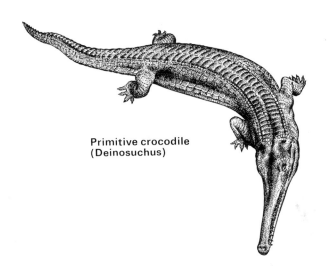

Primitive crocodile
(Deinosuchus)

Sauropod A large, or very large four-legged plant-eating dinosaur. See Sauropoda in the dictionary.

Sedimentary rock A kind of rock that has formed from mud or sand, such as mudstone, sandstone or limestone.

Seed ferns A group of plants that looked like ferns but which reproduced by seeds, rather than by spores.

Segnosaur A strange kind of meat-eating dinosaur. See Segnosauria in the dictionary.

Skeleton The bony framework that holds your body up (and which held up the bodies of the dinosaurs).

Species A group of animals which all look the same and can breed with each other. Human beings form one species. So do horses, alligators and so on.

Stegosaur An armoured dinosaur with bony plates on its back. See Stegosauria in the dictionary.

Thecodontians A member of the group includes the ancestor of the dinosaurs and crocodiles.

Triassic The first geological period in the age of the dinosaurs, from 245 to 205 million years ago.

Warm-blooded An animal that can control its body temperature to a set level, such as a bird or a mammal.

Index

184

ACKNOWLEDGEMENTS

9 Dinosaur National Monument, Utah; 17 Institute of Geological Sciences; 128 left Imitor, right Imitor; 129 Imitor; 131 top Imitor, bottom Mansell Collection; 132 P. Morris; 133 Imitor; 134 Imitor; 135 Museum Naturkund, Berlin; 137 Xinhua News Agency; 138–139 Michael Benton; 140 Imitor; 141 Courtesy, Field Museum of Natural History, Chicago; 147 Michael Chinery; 149 American Meteorite Laboratory; 156 Picturepoint; 158 Imitor; 162 Senkenberg Museum; 169 Imitor; 171 Calgary Natural History Park; 172 P. Morris; 173 P. Morris

Picture Research: Jackie Cookson